ELLE RUSS

CONFIDENT

AS

FU*K

D1510096

* **How to ditch bad vibes, clean up your past, and cultivate
confidence in order to make your dreams a reality**

FROM THE MADISON LIBRARY

renee hancox

FROM THE MADISON LIBRARY

Leslie Richter

Copyright © August 22 2019 by Elle Russ. All Rights Reserved.

Except as permitted under the United States Copyright Act of 1976, reproduction or utilization of this work in any form or by any electronic, mechanical, or other means, now known or hereafter invented, including xerography, photocopying, and recording, and in any information storage and retrieval system, is forbidden without written permission of the author and publisher. Mention of specific companies, organizations, or authorities in this book does not imply endorsement by the author or publisher. Neither the author nor the publisher assumes any responsibility for errors, omissions, or contrasting interpretations of the subject matter herein. Any per-ceived slight of any individual or organization is purely unintentional. Some names and identifying details have been changed to protect the privacy of individuals. The author received no incentives or compen-sation to promote the item recommendations in the book.

ISBN: 978-1-695-35968-0

Library of Congress Control Number: 1-7994448222

DISCLAIMER: The ideas, concepts, and opinions expressed in this book are intended to be used for entertainment and educational purposes only. This book is sold with the understanding that the author and publisher are not rendering psychological advice or medical advice of any kind, nor is this book intended to replace medical or psychological advice, nor to diagnose, prescribe, or treat any disease, condition, illness, or injury. The author and publisher claim no responsibility to any person or entity for any liability, loss, or damage caused or alleged to be caused directly or indirectly as a result of the use, application, or interpretation of the material in this book.

Editing: Ashleigh VanHouten
Cover Design: Janee Meadows
Back Cover Photo: Jonathan Moeller Photography
Publisher: Elle Russ (www.ElleRuss.com)

CONTENTS

I dedicate this book to my incredible mother, who firmly instructed me as a child: "Never let anyone, not even an adult, speak down to you or patronize you. Remember to always take your mouth with you—speak up." Mom, I love you more than anything in this entire world, and I am taking my mouth with me.

ACKNOWLEDGMENTS

I am so grateful for:

The Sisson Family: Mark, Carrie, Devyn, Kyle, Shanti, Ninja, and Jedi. Words cannot fully express the depths of how much I love each and every one of you. Thank you for believing in me, and for being wonderful, loving, hilarious beings.

Michael Bloom: My best friend since high school—thank you for encouraging and supporting me through thick and thin. Love you.

Dr. David T. Bowen, MD: For over a decade of helping me with my hand injury and for possessing the strength of vulnerability to comfort me emotionally.

Dr. Gary E. Foresman, MD: For believing in me, encouraging me, and for being the best doctor anyone could ever wish for.

To all of my coaching clients, podcast listeners, readers, and social media friends: thank you so much for all of the positive feedback and for supporting my mission over the years. I have learned so much from each and every one of you!

FOREWORD

I've had a close personal and business relationship with Elle Russ for many years, and I am excited to introduce her breakthrough new book to you. A few years ago, Elle shared with me her dream of writing a book like this, profane title and all! The clarity, enthusiasm, and conviction was stunning. I strongly encouraged her to go for it, and I have looked forward to the release day since then. Elle is a free thinker, free spirit, and an incredibly passionate and energetic human being. With the bookstores and your bookshelves crowded with so many books, I can assure you that this one will stand out from the pack and glow back at you, beckoning you to take an amazing journey with Elle.

As you might be able to discern from the title, this is not yet another self-help book filled with platitudes, acronyms and tidy to-do lists. This is a raw, unfiltered swing for the fences on the touchy topics of self-esteem, self-confidence, and shattering barriers that are in the way of authentically cultivating these esteemed personal attributes. I love how Elle shares her personal story with deep conviction and vulnerability to engage you, but always keeps her eye on you—the reader—to give you something valuable and actionable to implement in your own life. We have enough people on social media shining the spotlight on themselves and telling feel-good stories that provide a brief burst of entertainment and inspiration at best, and are pandering at worst. This book is different, deeper, and more powerful.

Elle's valiant battle against debilitating injury and medical challenges has framed her professional life into one dedicated to helping others—both healing and nourishing the physical body and also nurturing the spirit. This book will help you help yourself, but you are going to have to do the hard work and the deep reflection. Elle is not about subtlety, soft touches, or nuance. She is dedicated to excellence, transformation, and never looking back, feeling sorry for herself, or turning away from a challenge!

Congratulations for taking the huge step of buying this book, which tells me that you have an open mind, a sense of humor, a willingness to challenge fixed beliefs and give new ideas a try. Have a great journey with Elle!

Mark Sisson
October 2019
Miami Beach, FL

INTRODUCTION

Life is not easy for any of us. But what of that? We must have perseverance and above all confidence in ourselves. We must believe that we are gifted for something, and that this thing, at whatever cost, must be attained.

– **Marie Curie**

My friends were not surprised that I was writing a book on confidence. My entire life has followed a pattern of attracting friends, strangers, and work colleagues who need a helping hand with confidence, self-esteem, self-compassion, and speaking up. I have not merely been a cheerleader and coach to these people, because all of them have taught me valuable lessons in return. While I am *Confident As Fu*k* and truly one of the most confident people I know, confident people often need assistance in the following areas: vulnerability, active listening, compromise, addiction to struggle, kindness, diplomacy, and receiving.

Whether you are shy and seeking to gain confidence, or you are ultra-confident and need to refine that confidence and self-esteem, my intention in writing this book is that you will be inspired to take control of your life and step into a new, polished, perfectly *Confident As Fu*k* version of you. It is worth the effort to get there because confidence applies to every area of our lives, from the boardroom to the bedroom and everywhere in between.

While there are different connotations for the terms confidence and self-esteem, my use of the term *Confident As Fu*k* is meant to be all-encompassing. You can be confident and have low self-esteem or have high self-esteem but lack confidence. Becoming *Confident As Fu*k* is about having both, not one without the other.

All of my opinions are based on my experiences and observations in life. While there are research studies mentioned in my conversation with Mark Leary Ph.D., I am not offering you a textbook riddled with statistics and studies involving confidence—but instead, a more intimate and relatable portrait of examples from my life and others' lives so you can resonate with illustrations of real-life human interactions and ways of thinking.

My *Confident As Fu*k* nature has not been attained without several blows to it over the years, and at times my confidence needed repairing, refining, and course-correction. Confidence is yours to possess no matter where you are now. I have seen confidence spring up from the deepest wells of self-sabotage, dreadfully low self-esteem, and debilitating shyness. If you attend to it, confidence and self-esteem continually grows and gets better as the years go by. Life is shorter than we want it to be; it's time to step out of the shadows and start standing in the foreground with immense self-esteem and confidence. It's time to become *Confident As Fu*k*.

PART 1

DECONSTRUCTING CONFIDENCE

WHAT IS CONFIDENCE?

Confidence is not some fixed, anchored quality within you; your levels of confidence are always the sum of the thoughts you think and the actions you take. It is not reflective of your actual capacity to succeed at something, but more reflective of your *belief in your ability to prevail* at life in general or a specific endeavor. Since you can change your thoughts and actions, confidence and self-esteem is within your power. Even the most shy people crippled by fear can attain it through self-awareness, intention, practice, and perseverance.

Having confidence provides an evolutionary edge of sorts. It helps us navigate new challenges, tasks, and social situations without pause, anxiety, or fear, thus propelling us in the direction of accomplishing our goals and realizing our dreams.

Truly confident people with high self-esteem exemplify these characteristics:

* They approach challenging situations as something to be conquered and mastered, not hazards to be feared or avoided
* They are comfortable with failures and mistakes
* They speak with authority
* They are dependable, reliable, trustworthy, and on time
* They encourage, foster, and celebrate the success of others
* They take initiative

* They are leaders
* They are decisive
* They are goal-oriented
* They focus on their strengths, not weaknesses
* They have healthy relationships
* They have self-compassion
* They are not easily offended
* They have the ability to laugh at themselves
* They choose reason over reaction
* They are constantly learning
* They are loving and compassionate towards others
* They believe in their own abilities
* They use effective communication skills
* They feel loved and valued by those around them
* They do not feel the need to prove themselves to anyone
* They have defined, and are achieving, their own definition of success
* They are happy
* They speak the truth as they see it: they tell it like it is
* They don't care much what other people think of them
* They handle stressful situations with composure and ease
* They focus on the solution rather than dwell on the problem
* They face uncertainty with fortitude, not fear

CONFIDENCE IS YOUR BIRTHRIGHT

The only opponent is yourself.

- **Erin Fall Haskell,** *Awakening*

Babies and little children automatically draw boundaries in honor of their self-esteem by making demands, almost declaring their worth by screaming "No." A child raised with unconditional love can flourish and develop confidence, but sometimes lose it along the journey of life. Where does it all go wrong? Perhaps a teacher in second grade labeled you a slow reader, or a family member labeled you as the dummy of the household. Labels, projections, stories, and more labels. My fifth-grade math teacher used to yell at us with a fearful tone, "If you don't become proficient at math, you will all be sweeping floors at the local theme park when you grow up!" I dislike math and thus was not proficient in it because I don't care about being good at it, and I am not currently sweeping floors at any establishments. My grade school science teacher uttered a similar sentiment about the importance of being proficient at science, and I received terrible grades in science as a student yet eventually wrote a bestselling book involving science. Hey teachers: stop instilling fearful nonsense and doomsday prophesies in your students' subconscious.

Continually warding off the bombardment of other people's projections— being bullied in school, having relationships with controlling people— can be a challenge; we can easily evolve from a naturally confident creature into a fearful, self-doubting teenager and adult. Unless you catch your inner thoughts and limiting beliefs about your confidence and then course-correct, your life will feel like riding a rogue train to insecurity island—an altogether unpleasant existence. We were designed to be confident, and it is time to own your birthright.

PARENTAL GARBAGE

It is possible to emerge from the sub-par parenting you were subjected to and *parent yourself* into greatness. It's true, the way we were raised can immensely shape the way we see ourselves as adults. The child who was told he would amount to nothing either soars to success or he succumbs to a story created by someone else. My purpose is you show you how to untangle this mess and start to cultivate your own stories and projections about yourself. If you really think about it, it's pretty insane to allow someone else's story or opinion of you to alter how *you think about you.* Conversely, everyone around you could be encouraging and loving, yet you are telling yourself a defeating story that is holding you back in life. Either way, you are the hero or enemy in the pursuit of your own happiness and success.

BRANDON'S STORY

Brandon is 40 years old. In his household growing up he was always labeled the "brat," the one who defied authority. Brandon's father always made him out to be wrong. Once, his father could not find the hammer in the toolbox and accused Brandon of taking it. Brandon truthfully had no idea where it was. When his father ultimately found the hammer, he never apologized to Brandon for accusing him. Crap like this would happen throughout Brandon's childhood and he would get blamed for things he didn't do, and when Brandon became a contractor as an adult, his childhood story would play out on his jobs. It would always follow this pattern:

Something would go wrong on the job.

Brandon would get blamed by the authority on the job even

when it wasn't his fault, and he would often get yelled at in a patronizing way by his boss in front of his co-workers.

Brandon would not defend himself, but instead cower under authority and feel bad about himself. He then felt anxious and fearful about future contracts.

I said to Brandon, "This career-pattern does not happen to me ever, or anyone else that I know, so let's get to the bottom of this because the common denominator is *you*. Is there anything like this that would happen in your house while growing up?"

Brandon's childhood pattern made perfect sense, and he was continually replaying familiar patterns with people in positions of authority. Brandon knew that he had to break this string of bad work experiences and attract better ones into his life. He started to understand that *he was not wrong. He did not have to be wrong.*

After digging through this self-inquiry minefield, Brandon emerged believing that he could change his future experiences, and he did a 180-degree turnaround. The first order of business was preparing Brandon to stand up to the moody, high-tempered bosses he often worked for. Brandon cultivated the self-esteem and confidence to plan the following: The next time he was yelled at and blamed for something that was not his fault on a job, he was prepared to speak up for himself—something to the effect of, "I am not going to be spoken to like that again, so unless you change your tone right now and start speaking to me like a human being, I will walk out on this job." Granted, Brandon had prepared himself beforehand to lose the job and get fired for standing his ground, but that didn't happen. In fact, what happened was a classic outcome of calling a bully on their shit. The bully (Brandon's boss) acquiesced in the face of being stood up to. The boss apologized, and never did it again.

Brandon had a few more jobs with the same bully and things

went smoothly, but Brandon ultimately moved on from working with that boss and no longer had to experience jobs with patronizing personalities in charge. In fact, for the first time in his adult life, Brandon started to attract the opposite. He began to work with respectful, appreciative bosses who praised him for jobs well done, and Brandon started to have contracts where *nothing went wrong*! Only once in the five years following his epiphany was his new-found self-esteem tested by one slightly negative work experience. He stood up for himself one more time, but beyond that exception, the remaining jobs he worked on were blissful and he was always appreciated and showered with praise. In my experience, witnessing many scenarios like Brandon's, it seems like the universe throws us a few test-situations once we have overcome a difficult long-term pattern; it's almost like a refresher course saying, "Just checking in to confirm that you learned this lesson in self-esteem and confidence." Thanks but no thanks for the crappy gift, Dad—I just tossed it into the trash, and good riddance! What a difference self-examination and intention can make.

I have had the opposite experiences of Brandon with employment. I have never been fired from a job, nor have I ever been reprimanded by a boss. Everything in my work-life has gone well, in fact brilliantly well. I am always appreciated and promoted. Is this because I am luckier, more talented, or more skilled than Brandon? I don't believe that. We both just had different thoughts and feelings about ourselves with regards to employment: my high self-esteem and confidence in that area attracted more of the same. Brandon's low self-esteem and lack of confidence in that area brought him more of the same as well. No more of that for Brandon, or for you. This stuff is fixable.

I've heard that abused children will sometimes reach out for and cry for their abusive parent while being removed by police officers for child abuse. That is all that child knows. It is *familiar*. It is not healthy, in fact it is terribly sad, but it is all that abused child knows of a relationship between a parent and child. It's human nature: we are sometimes drawn to what is familiar, even when it is destructive.

Why do some people continually attract mentally or physically abusive romantic partners into their lives? Why would anyone keep returning to a person who abuses them? It often stems from *what is familiar to them*. Perhaps they watched a parent be abused or perhaps their first romantic experience involved mental or physical abuse, thus igniting a pattern that led to trust issues in dating and a subconscious belief that they were not worthy of something better. Perhaps a teenage girl came home crying to her mother after being hit by a boyfriend and the mother reacted with, "Well, what did you do to make him mad?" You can see how the imprinting happens. While tragic, these patterns and programs can be changed. Low self-esteem and lack of confidence can lead to unpleasant life experiences that perpetuate. We need to take control over our thoughts and emotions and get to work on trudging through this dumpster fire of childhood nonsense.

By the way, if you have ever been mentally or physically abused by anyone, let me *parent you* now and say this: fuck them. You are better than allowing that piece of garbage from the past to continue abusing you...*by you allowing that imprinted experience of the past to continue to harm you*. Are you really going to let that person be right about their story of you and essentially succeed at taking you down? No, you are not. No way they get to win—*you* get to win. I don't care who you are, I believe in your ability to prevail. You are wired to win; own that birthright.

MY OWN CHILDHOOD-TO-ADULTHOOD GARBAGE

I am *Confident As Fu*k.* However, when we talk about childhood experiences that can affect our self-esteem as adults, my experiences in childhood attracted issues in one specific area: romantic relationships with men. My father was a very funny guy, cool and smart, but he was a drunk. A nice drunk, a fun drunk, but still a drunk. He was never mean, verbally or physically abusive, and he loved hanging out with his kids. He was proud of me. He had a lot of great qualities that I am grateful for and proud of. Nonetheless, being an alcoholic ultimately led him to drop the ball on our family.

My father spiraled and ultimately lost all of our money when I was in fifth grade. After years of struggling with an alcoholic and having to pick up the pieces, my mother finally left him. Her hope was that after she left, he would finally get his act together for the sake of our family. She waited. He never did. She divorced him a few years later.

My father was from a wealthy, highly educated, successful family. Everything looked perfect with the Russ'. My grandparents had a beautiful mansion with tennis courts and a swimming pool, and my father and his sister attended summer camps in Switzerland and traveled the world first-class at a time when not many people had the means to do so. My father and his relatives seemed like a lovely family to be a part of, and my parents decided early on that my mother would stay at home and raise the children while my dad worked and supported the family. Everything seemed happy and secure: their love, their finances, and their future. Until it wasn't.

As a kid, witnessing my alcoholic father lose all of our money was painfully embarrassing. My mother had to step up and financially support her children and it felt so unfair to watch her struggle with no help from my dad. So, the story I spoke aloud to others (and thought silently) when it came to men was this: "Don't be fooled.

You can meet a guy and everything looks great–they have a great education, money, potential, a good family and they promise to take care of you—and one day, boom! You are left in the dust with nothing. You can't count on them."

And so, with that revelation-declaration I set out to become as financially independent as possible so I could bypass the façade of a secure life offered by a dude who would ultimately fail me—perhaps even become a drunken loser—and then leave me in the dust to pick up the pieces. You will not be surprised as to what I attracted romantically: men who could not be counted on. It showed up in a variety of ways, whether it was a boyfriend who cheated (untrustworthy) or a man who wasn't interested in having a serious relationship (unavailable), or men who needed to be rescued, men who lacked ambition to provide, men with no potential, and so on.

Finally, one day I noticed that this kind of junk didn't happen to my friends. Some of their relationships didn't work out, but they never experienced the kind of issues that I did. I was indeed the common denominator in this painful pattern. It was a very sad day realizing that my original belief about not being able to trust men was killing my soul and affecting my future romantic prospects. I realized that all of my close male friends embodied what I wanted in a man. I chose all of my male friends really well, but somehow I did not apply the same standards to my romantic partners. I had wonderful examples of good men all around me, yet I was continually manifesting disaster boyfriends.

After this conclusion, I got to work on myself and I dug deep. I finally began attracting men who were ambitious, reliable, and trustworthy. I did get a refresher course by the universe, of course; I was brought one more piece of garbage whom I ditched quickly after discovering that he was part of my old pattern. Two months with garbage is better than two years or a lifetime, though. We're all a work in progress.

(One additional and critical component I eventually solved was dealing with shame combined with learning to be vulnerable. Later in this book, I share how my Achilles heel—a physical disability I sustained at the age of 22—led to my attracting emotionally unavailable men and what I did to course-correct that piece of the puzzle.)

THE DOWNER EFFECT

No one can make you feel inferior without your consent.

– **Eleanor Roosevelt**

Aside from the thoughts you think about yourself, you have self-defeating thoughts about others. It's negative and unbecoming of who you are on the inside, which is a person who *does not want those same thoughts, thought about you.* When we think shitty, unsupportive thoughts about others, those judgements never feel good, and it decreases our own self-esteem and levels of confidence. I'm down with OPC (Other People's Confidence). Stop interfering and messing with other people's confidence unless you want yours to be messed with.

It is a valid exercise to pinpoint how and why you feel yucky sometimes (or all the time) after hanging out with certain people, even friends and family members. I am going to put my middle finger on it. I call it The Downer Effect. And before you start ripping on people you know who are downers, at some point you were also guilty of being a downer and don't even realize it. I am guilty of it too.

DOWNER EFFECT #1

Here is a simple example of the downer effect. I love the island of Maui. One of the numerous nature attractions is driving 10,000 feet up to the Haleakalā Crater (a dormant volcano) to watch the sunrise. One day, I decided to do it. I am really efficient at managing time and I am always early or right on time—never late. I knew exactly how much time it would take me to reach the summit from the base. When I pulled up in my car to the park ranger station which is eleven miles from the actual summit, the park ranger said to me, "Are you here to watch the sunrise?" "Yes, I am!" I replied with excitement. He said, "You're never going to make it in time."

I told him that I was going to attempt it anyway and I paid the park entrance fee. After I pulled away from the ranger station I thought to myself, "Bullshit, I am totally going to make it." Not only did I make it on time, I had the perfect amount of time to spare. In fact, had I gotten to the summit earlier than I did, I might have been freezing cold and uncomfortable because it was 50 degrees up there. Instead, I had enough time to park, get cozy, find the perfect spot to watch the sunrise...and I waited only five minutes for the sun to rise up through the clouds. It was beautiful. I really wanted to drive back down the crater afterwards and shout, "Hey ranger, I made it—stop being a deputy downer!"

I could have listened to the ranger and turned around and given up on my sunrise excursion, but I didn't. I wonder how many people missed a once-in-a-lifetime experience because of that ranger? I had more confidence in my time management that I had confidence in his opinion. This is just a minor example of the downer effect, a simple one to illustrate that downers are all around us, even at the park ranger station in Maui. What could the ranger have said to be less of a downer? How about saying nothing—or something like, "You might be cutting it close on time to see the sunrise, but it's worth a shot and it is beautiful up there regardless." Anything other than, "Nope, you're never gonna make it." Aloha, downer.

DOWNER EFFECT #2

Candace's assistant manager quit at a time when she had an immense workload. Her employee quit because he was offered Candace's exact position and title at another company, a big promotion up the corporate ladder for him. Frustrated, Candace told me all of the reasons why her soon-to-be ex-employee was not qualified for that job: "He is way in over his head, he doesn't have the skills or the knowledge for this job. He will be managing thirty people! He was good at managing a small number of people, but he is way over his head on this." Then Candace snipped, "Just watch, he won't be able to hack it and he'll come begging for his old job back, trust me."

Wowzers. Candace was secretly hoping he would fail in his new position! Why would Candace want him to fail? So she could be right and have an "I told you so" moment, even if she only muttered it to herself? I posed a couple of questions: "What if the company he is going to had someone less capable than him in the position, and he gets in there and impresses the hell out of them? Or, what if he just kicks ass at the job way more than his predecessor and becomes a superstar?" Both were possible. Even though Candace never expressed her thoughts to his face, she was being a downer. You might ask, "So what? Why would it matter what her private thoughts were about that person?"

It matters. Whether or not you believe in the power of intention, the power of the subconscious mind, the law of attraction, energy, quantum mechanics, Jesus, or aliens, when you emit a negative vibe, other people pick up on it. It's universally clear: you know damn well when someone is vibrating negative energy and thoughts towards you. You can just feel it. We all can. Think about the negative energy Candace was putting out there towards her ex-employee. She was hoping he would fail and have to come groveling back in shame and embarrassment, begging for his old job back. Suddenly she hated this guy, but simultaneously didn't want to lose him as an employee? Would you want her to be your boss?

When you take a deeper look behind annoying emotions and feelings of anger or jealousy, you'll see that you have the opportunity to change your thoughts and emotions. Here's the deal though: you, me, Candace, and everyone we know has thoughts like these. You might still have them. But *Confident As Fu*k* people do not truly wish for and revel in other people's misfortunes.

I told Candace, "How about changing your thinking to, 'Ok, I don't really believe in his abilities in his new job and I am sitting here hoping he fails. Let me turn this around and start hoping he does well and rises to the challenge, and succeeds. Why wouldn't I want him to succeed? He has been a great assistant manager and I like the guy. I don't really want him to fail, do I? I am just inconvenienced by him quitting right now and I reacted as if I were being attacked. That is just my ego, and if I really think about it, he deserves to move up in his career. It's never a good time for someone to quit, but we all have to take opportunities when they show up."

Candace changed her entire attitude instantly. She said, "You're right, it's true—I don't truly want him to fail at all. If I really think about it, I hope he succeeds in his new position."

The emotional charge was removed for Candace, and the immediate effect was her feeling better instead of aggravated—a step in the right direction. She saw how she was being a downer, and her newfound support for her employee brought a new energy into the office the next day at work. Instead of Candace emanating an air of, "Good luck asshole, you'll be back," she walked into the office full of well-wishes and encouragement. Isn't that an all-around better life experience for everybody? Candace learned a year later that her ex-employee completely rose to the new challenge, kicked major butt in his new position, and impressed the hell out of everybody. Turns out Candace was dead-wrong in her initial downer reaction—he was a superstar after all.

Whenever you shake your head about another person and say to yourself sarcastically, "Yeah right, good luck with that," you are being a downer. Whether or not it is spoken, those negative thoughts are wrapped up with judgement about how someone else lives their life and their capabilities. And when you judge someone else it usually doesn't feel good. I guarantee that if you knew someone was thinking the same kind of thoughts about you that Candace was, you would declare, "What an asshole!" So, stop thinking that way about other people.

How would you feel if you could read a person's mind and they were doubting you in their minds? You would feel betrayed. So why would you do it to others, even silently? Give your friends, family, and strangers the benefit of the doubt, and the moment you start shaking your head in judgement, just turn it around and think, "Alright, hold on here, right now I am being a downer about this person's life, and I am going to sit here and reframe my thoughts until I can honestly wish them the best and envision them success-ful in their endeavor. I hope they prove me wrong." Why do this? Because it nice. Don't be a dick. Don't be a downer friend. It is more likely that that kind of negative thinking will backfire on you. Those negative emotions are hurting you, not your intended target.

DOWNER EFFECT #3

Here's another seemingly innocuous downer scenario. I admit it: I'm not a fan of road cycling. Every time I used to see a cyclist on the stretch of the Pacific Coast Highway, I would think to myself, "Ugh, what a moron." Not only because they are cycling dangerously close to cars and that freaks me out, but because I just personally don't enjoy cycling. I find it to be the most uncomfortable and un-ergonomic position for my body and I think those spandex outfits are universally unflattering. For years, every time I passed a cyclist in my car I would shake my head and think, "Idiot."

Here's the truth about my seemingly innocuous downer thought. I would be driving along the ocean in a completely happy, positive state just prior to seeing a cyclist, and then boom! I would morph into judgment mode and kill my own positive vibe. I am the idiot in that scenario, not the cyclist. One day while driving, I had the following thought: I love stand up paddling on the ocean, and I bet you there is a cyclist who rides down Pacific Coast Highway and sees paddlers like me on the ocean and thinks, "What a moron, paddling out there with sharks. Idiot!"

My close friends still joke about my cycling prejudice, but now when I pass a cyclist on the road, I laugh at my former negative thoughts about them, and if my old downer ways get triggered, I immediately say to myself, "Hey. Stop dipping into negativity and judging their sport! Not everyone likes the same sports, some people hate swimming and you love swimming. To each their own. Enough with the judgements. You are letting a stranger and their sports equipment put you in a negative state."

When you break down and really translate that flippant commentary in your head, you can see what an asshole downer you are being—and how it benefits no one, including yourself.

DOWNER EFFECT #4

My career endeavors and goals have been the target of downer energy numerous times. For example, a stranger might ask me what I do for work. I do many things, but I usually keep it simple and say, "I am a writer." Once, a stranger responded very skeptically, "So, are you like a *real writer who makes money at it* or are you a writer who goes and writes at Starbucks but actually has another job?" "Wow," I responded, "That's a fucked-up response. Would you ask a real estate agent, 'So, are you like a *real* real estate agent who makes money selling houses, or do you just have a real estate license but actually make money at something else?'" He rolled his eyes defensively and responded, "Well, that's different." I said, "It's not different at all, dude. It's rude. But luckily for me, every time a person like you says some negative downer shit like that to me, it only exponentially increases my success. So, mahalo."

People in creative professions may get more downer reactions from strangers and loved ones than nearly any other profession. Here's another response I get: "Geez, must be really tough to be a writer, I mean it's so competitive and so hard to be successful at." I responded, "It's not tough or competitive for all of the published authors and other writers out there who are currently successful at it. Not hard for them at all."

Let's say you tell a friend that you want to start a business and they warn, "Okay, but be careful because 50 percent of new businesses fail." My response would be, "I don't give a shit about your statistics, because I choose to be on the side of the 50 percent of people who *succeed at it.*"

If I used statistics or took to heart the public's impression of how hard and competitive creative professions were, I would never have helped thousands of people around the world regain their health with my first book, *The Paleo Thyroid Solution*. In hindsight, should I have listened to what these downers had to say about what was realistic or tough to accomplish? Hell no. Thankfully I didn't listen, and you shouldn't either.

DOWNER EFFECT #5

When I was a freshman in high school, two fellow teenagers wanted to be television and film actresses in Hollywood. One night they came over to our place for a gathering and they were both talking about moving to Los Angeles to pursue their Hollywood dreams. I distinctly recall sitting in front of these girls and thinking to myself, "Yeah right, good luck with that Hollywood dream, you two will be flying back home in no time."

Well, in my downer face. They did it: they both became famous and rich and respected for their acting talents. I got a further taste of my own medicine when I pursued the same career in the entertainment industry many years later and experienced people making similar downer comments, or exuding that same look that I knew all too well—the look that says, "Yeah right, good luck with that." I got my ass handed to me on that one about 15 years later. Good one, universe.

Always err on the side of wishing people achieve their dreams. The more you feel it for other people (even if unspoken) the more you will feel the same support come your way, whether from your current social network or new people who will show up and encourage you and even assist you in achieving your goals. I have an alternative spin on a quote originally attributed to a Finnish composer named Jean Sibelius who said, "No one ever built a statue to a critic." My spin on it is, "No one ever built a statue of a skeptic."

Have you ever seen a statute of a person where the description read, "This guy believed in nothing and was always skeptical of the stuff everyone else suggested was possible"? No, you haven't, because we erect statutes to honor people who lead the charge and believe in something others think impossible. We honor heroes in our world who go above and beyond what's considered possible and prove to us that it can be done. They conquered something. This goes for your life as well. Maybe you want to be an opera singer but, "It's too competitive and so hard to get a talent agent." The longer you continue to simmer in skepticism, the longer you hold yourself back from the unknown, unmeasurable, unforeseen probabilities that are possible in your life. There are likely several probabilities you have already missed out on because you were a skeptic focused on statistics and what the majority considers realistic.

DOWNER EFFECT #6

When it came time for me to pitch *The Paleo Thyroid Solution* to Mark Sisson with the hope that he would offer me a book deal, I was mentioning to a family member that I had written an extensive book outline and was excited about pitching it to Mark. This family member, with a tone of great skepticism said, "But, you have never written a book before." That comment could easily have punched a hole in my self-esteem and confidence. Instead, it fueled me, and I responded with, "That is inconsequential, I have written many things in my life already. A book is just a different format. It's that simple."

After I got the book deal, I was speaking with that same family member and I mentioned that Mark agreed to publish my book. Again, they said in a very skeptical tone, "Well, now you have to *actually write it.*" Their tone was obvious: they did not have the confidence in me that I could execute it. What a downer.

Before my book was published, a prominent bookstore pre-ordered 1,000 copies of my book and I relayed this good news to the same family member. As you can probably guess, I received another downer response. This time they sort of laughed in a mocking tone, "Well, that seems silly. I mean, they haven't even read your book yet; why would they buy copies of something they haven't even read?" Now this person was projecting that my book would be crap, that the bookstore would be regretful of their decision, and I would end up looking like a fool. They were essentially relegating me to a future where I didn't show up and I couldn't pull it off. These kinds of comments come at you from all over the place, even from loved ones. After my book was published and successful, I went back to that family member and spoke honestly about their problematic comments. When I broke it down, they understood and felt bad about it, and they expressed how it wasn't their intention—but they understood how those comments were massively unsupportive.

I was talking to a close friend who has never written anything before, and as I was in the midst of writing *The Paleo Thyroid Solution*, she called me in a parental-like panic akin to overseeing a child's science project that was due in 24 hours. She said, "What's up? Are you writing? How far along are you? Are you working on it?" Her tone implied that I was not only somehow slacking in my commitment to writing the book, but that she was worried I might not finish it.

I said, "Hey dude, I have always finished projects that I have started. I have never said I was going to do a thing and then didn't do it. You know this about me. So, while *you may not be able to imagine yourself writing a book*, don't project your insecurities and lack of confidence onto me. I am writing my book and I don't need you, especially you, to be over my shoulder telling me to do it, because I am already self-motivated. So, please stop the negative commentary because you are being a major downer."

She instantly got the message loud and clear. She is still a close friend. In many years of friendship, we have maybe had three moments like this. We can be direct and honest with each other because we are both confident people with high self-esteem and we can accept a tell-it-like-it-is mic drop from each other without being offended (one of the many benefits of having friends who are confident!). Besides, she is not usually a downer, she was just having a downer moment and needed that pointed out. She accepted it and apologized. I have also been a downer and willing to accept heat for it. I welcome it. If you are truly my friend, please call me on my shit.

It's inevitable: strangers and loved ones are going to project their lack of confidence in a subject onto your confidence in a subject; how are you going to get through that? Are you just going to let these people tell you something about yourself you don't believe? Are you going to let them have a stake in your success? The above naysayers were a close friend and a family member who both love me. At the core, they do believe in me. They are awesome. But they are not immune from being downers on occasion. At every turn in writing my first book I encountered the downer effect from strangers and loved ones. The difference is, I let it fuel my confidence, not hinder it. Let downers in your life fuel *your* confidence. It is not about proving them wrong, it is about proving yourself awesome.

You cannot care about what anyone else thinks of your goals. All that matters is what you think of them. If I didn't hold this philosophy, I would never have achieved any of my goals. When you are confident, you are confident in your ability to prevail, confident in your ethics, and confident in your approach to people. Do not listen to what anyone else has to say about your dreams or your abilities. It only matters what *you think of you.*

DOWNER EFFECT #7

I have a friend in their 40s who has never had health insurance. This topic is personal to me because I have been the beneficiary of insurance and I was raised with the philosophy that you never go without it, because you never know when something could happen and you might need it (a common philosophy about health insurance). I was trying to convince my friend to finally get health insurance and she responded with, "I don't have any fears about my health, Elle. I don't worry about walking outside of my house without health insurance like you and others do." Frustrated by what I considered an insane response, I kept trying to convince her that she was being dumb about this and she really needed to buy health insurance. I gave all sorts of examples, even from my own life when insurance saved me. She didn't budge at all, she just kept telling me that she wasn't worried about her health. After we ended the call, I was shaking my head and totally judging her life. I had the following thought, "Watch...something is going to happen and she'll see what an idiot she was."

Let's unpack that downer reaction, shall we? In order for me to be right and her be wrong, something really, really bad would have to happen to her. Think about it: if the lesson I wanted to teach her and be right about (how not having insurance could screw a person financially) then she would have to A) have a health situation pop up, and B) it would have to be so bad that it left her financially strained beyond what she could afford. My desire to win an argument on the benefits of health insurance would also mean that I want something bad health-wise to happen to my friend. Imagine if you knew that a friend of yours had the same thoughts about you, essentially wishing you a tragic health failure of some kind. I would be mortified if a friend of mine had those same thoughts about me, yet there I was, wishing a tragic medical story upon her! It was just a thought, but thoughts matter and they are worth unraveling and translating when associated with negative emotions. I would rather have my life filled with supportive, happy thoughts about my friends rather than secretly hoping one of them falls off a cliff so I could have a private, *I told you so* moment.

Next time you are feeling adamant about being right, check yourself to see if your thoughts are related to a negative outcome for another person. Most of us have had thoughts like this, and still do. That's okay, it's the negative side of ego popping up, but the important thing is to catch it when possible, turn it around, and start emanating a different vibration, a different energy. You know when to catch yourself because your emotions will tell you something is off. I was angry and frustrated when I got off the phone with her and felt the need to be right; those were my indicators to unpack those feelings and rightfully conclude that I was the downer. Wishing ill-will and failure upon someone is just another stumbling block to becoming *Confident As Fu*k* yourself. Turn it around and wish success and good health upon others. It is a kinder way to think, especially about the people you call your friends.

DOWNER EFFECT #8

The following type of downer is everywhere. A friend takes a flight back into town after a trip, and the airline delays their flight and changes the terminal. We have all heard a lame airport story from someone (or told one ourselves). When they return and you ask how their trip was, they go into a water-cooler rant about the delayed flights and the lines at the airport. Look, no one wants to hear about your shitty customer service experience at the airport or the bank. Do you really need to share this one? Choose your vents wisely. And don't forget, in the retelling of your airport story, you regenerate the same feelings of aggravation that you felt while you were at the airport! Looks like the airport won control over your emotions. Knock it off.

DOWNER EFFECT #9

Someone told me a sensational story once, out of the blue, about their friend who was randomly stabbed in the back in New York City many years ago. Stabbed, for real, with a knife! Apparently this woman was unaware she had been stabbed until a few minutes later when she felt something weird and touched her back to discover blood. She was stabbed three times and never saw or felt anyone do it. Creepy! I was instantly horrified. That story immediately brought me down a rabbit hole of thinking about people who commit evil acts like that. Then I imagined the actual act of being stabbed three times in the back. I felt nauseous.

What a downer, right? And now I just told you the same downer story and sent you down a dark path of being immersed in the world of evildoers and physical trauma. See how it happens so easily from telling a fifteen-second story? Stop telling sensational, negative stories like this unless they serve some kind of specific purpose—otherwise it is just an exercise in spreading bad vibes to other people and bringing down the vibration of whatever conversation you were in the midst of. PS: Sorry I just told you that story, I know—it's a real fuckin' downer.

HOW TO AVOID DOWNERS

If you don't want downer vibes from people about your dreams and goals, only share them with people who will encourage you and support you. If no one around is supportive, hire an unbiased life coach to encourage you, or join a supportive online group, or encourage yourself until you feel confident enough to share with others.

It feels a lot better when you just zip it and not allow anyone else to offer a downer response that could alter your emotional state or dig at your confidence. I learned that every time I told a certain person in my life something I was excited about or interested in, he would give me all of the reasons why it might not work out. Over time, I stopped sharing things with him because I didn't like the downer commentary and lack of enthusiasm and encouragement. I moved away from that friendship. I exclusively share my goals and dreams with people in my life who get just as excited and hopeful about my ideas and plans as I do.

Let's say every time you tell your sister the exciting plans and dreams and goals you have, she shuts you down. At some point, you are the insane person for expecting a different outcome. How many times has this happened? Were you really expecting her to change her outlook? Your sister is just being herself: a person who does not support. If you keep getting responses and vibes you don't like from a person, stop engaging and stop hoping for it to change. At some point, you have no standing in feeling offended or upset about their non-supportive reactions, because you walked right into a known downer situation. I get it; we want the people around us and the people we love to be as excited as we are about our goals and plans. But they may never be, and that has to be okay with you. You must find other people to share it with who are supportive. More importantly, you have to generate the encouragement from within.

Places, people, and things that make you question your confidence and self-esteem—get rid of them or minimize them. Do you really need to keep talking to these people about your innermost desires? Stop answering calls; become too busy to hang out; fade-out on these people and situations. Stop being available for downers. One time I took my no-shit approach to a downer friend and said, "You know what Audrey, every time I talk to you it's one complaint or drama after another, and it never ends. It does not sound like you are happy about life at all. Perhaps you should start investigating how to be happy and live the life that you want, or seek out some coaching." That might sound harsh or it might not be your style, but I tell you what: at least that person understood why I stopped answering the phone as often, and I am better off for it.

PART
2

BECOMING
UNAVAILABLE

If you want to cultivate, increase, or fine-tune your self-esteem and confidence, you must start to become unavailable for certain people, situations, old ways of thinking, and engaging with others. You must become unavailable to your old self so that a new, *Confident As Fu*k* version can emerge.

NO MORE NONVERSATIONS

If you really want to be doing a thing, then you would be doing that thing or trying to do that thing...but just talking about it is doing NO THING.

- Elle Russ

Have you ever had conversations that feel like a royal waste of time? I call those NONversations: conversations that go nowhere.

A friend called me four years in a row complaining about being overweight and regretting his daily alcohol consumption. Every year he hatched a new plan to get healthy, but he never prevailed beyond a couple of weeks. Finally, I said, "Look, it's been four years in a row now that you've called me complaining about this stuff. From now on, you can have this NONversation with someone else, because I am unavailable to hear about it until you get off your ass and finally do something about it in a meaningful way. Stop saying you really want it, because you don't." Sometimes a brutal truth-kick in the ass can inspire someone to finally do the thing they keep saying they will do and stop dragging you in NONversations about it. In my experience, speaking up even when it is perceived as harsh is the thing that can move a person to change their circumstances. Does it matter whether they move into action because they want to prove you wrong? Who cares why they get motivated, if they get motivated. Tough love works.

I knew someone once who used to make the most illogical statements, and I would get frustrated and annoyed every time. For many years, every time Jane voiced an observation that I disagreed with strongly, I would try to argue back with reason and logic, but she was not on the same plane of awareness. Here's how it usually went: I would be annoyed at Jane's statement and try to explain why it was illogical, and then she would defend her position with even more illogical statements. This exchange would cause tension and negative energy in those moments. Over time, I realized the facts: *Jane is a person who says illogical shit. This is who she has been for more than 20 years.* I knew this about Jane, yet I still get annoyed? Who is the illogical person here? What was I expecting, that Jane would someday fully grasp my counterpoints to her statements? That is the definition of insanity.

I didn't have to see Jane often, so I decided to let her have her illogical conclusions. Instead of arguing or attempting to show her how irrational she was, I began ignoring it. My state of mind and emotions remained intact as I trained myself to no longer feel the need to convince Jane of anything, because it felt better to keep the peace than to become embroiled in a NONversation. Why insert discord into these rare in-person occurrences? I changed my response to either no response at all or, "Interesting point" or, "Hmm...never thought about it that way."

How about those who argue with or antagonize people on the internet about politics, religion, or other hot topics? Do you really think an agro-post on someone's social media page about politics or any other topic is going to change their opinion? More often than not, it won't. And let's be real, most of the time you are not interested in opening up a heartfelt philosophical debate, you are just publicly shaming the person and trying to prove why your opinion is better. All you're doing is creating a NONversation that will only raise the blood pressure and stress levels of both parties, which is very antagonistic to a happy existence. I have fallen into this trap a few times with a friend who has vastly different political and social policy views than I do, and I have been guilty of starting NONversations as if somehow I think this person is going to change their views suddenly? Insanity. Furthermore, I am only igniting those NONversations to push *my viewpoint.* Because no amount of debate can sway my beliefs about certain things, I am not opening up the floor for a thoughtful discussion. I basically just want to declare, "You are so wrong about this, and I am appalled that you believe this and think this way." Not only is it a waste of time, I regret every one of these interactions. So I stopped. It only leads to discord and aggravation and throws me out of a grateful, pleasant state of being. I don't wanna be *that guy,* and you shouldn't either. Check yourself next time you are caught up in a NONversation or instigating one.

YOUR VICTIM APPLICATION HAS BEEN DENIED

Confidence comes not from always being right but from not fearing to be wrong.

- Peter T. McIntyre

A 50-year-old woman bitterly complained to me about her current state of affairs:

"It just really pisses me off sometimes, because if my mother had just pushed me harder and motivated me more in life, I would be more successful."

I asked, "How long have you realized this about your mom?"

She said, "I don't know, probably when I turned thirty, I realized what she had done to me."

I responded: "Excuse me, but did I just hear you blame your mother for your adult life? If you knew this about your mother and yourself twenty years ago, why didn't *you* push and motivate *yourself* at some point? As an innocent child, your mother might have failed you, but you have been aware of your shortcomings for twenty years now? You better stop blaming your mother, because this is *your* fail now. You need to take responsibility. It's not her fault you don't feel successful in life, it's your fault."

It might seem easier to play the victim and blame our shortcomings and lack of confidence or success in life on the way we were parented, because then you don't have to take responsibility for your current lack of success or self-esteem or whatever else you feel is lacking in your life. But if we translate that behavior, it means you are letting another person (a parent), control your entire life—when really, you're doing it to yourself.

You have the capability and power to alter your perception and change your circumstances. People prevail in life despite terrible parenting. So how did they escape the throes of victimhood? Is it just a crapshoot? No, those people wanted it badly enough and did the inner work to get there. How badly do *you* want it? You can build self-worth, self-esteem, confidence, intelligence, or anything else you lacked from a parent or caregiver—even if you are so shy that you can barely talk to people. You are an adult now. It's time to take responsibility. You will change your life if you take ownership of it. If not, you can keep on letting crappy parenting *own you.* How is that working out for you? That's what I thought.

Mother yourself, or find someone else to help mother you. If you are 50 years old and still blaming your parents, you need to run to a therapist, a life coach, or a stack of self-improvement books. If you are more than 18 years old and conscious enough to see the negative effects of how you were raised, you can start to *raise yourself.* Otherwise, you are letting that shitty parent win, allowing them to have power over your success and happiness. You will be lying on your deathbed full of regrets, realizing in hindsight how you let someone else's opinions and treatment of you negatively affect your entire life. You only have one life on this earth, it's time to take control of it.

THERE ARE NO VICTIMS, ONLY VOLUNTEERS

You might be thinking, "Hey, I didn't volunteer for cancer!" or "Damn Elle, do you really think I volunteered to get mugged last Saturday on the subway?" No, anyone can be a victim of a situation. However, I would argue that if you repeatedly get mugged on the subway or you constantly get health problems, there might be something to look at within your past, your present, your current life, and the thoughts you think and stories you tell about yourself. I am not blaming anyone for getting a disease; I wrote a bestselling book about being jacked up for years with hypothyroidism, and I also have a permanent hand disability. I did not ask for either one of those. That being said, both of those physical issues led me to the most amazing experiences in life—so much so that I would never go back in time and choose a different path. If given the choice, I would choose the hand injury and the hypothyroidism again. I really would.

I have seen so many tragedies become the greatest gifts in people's lives, including my own. We are so quick to judge and define life's challenges without being open to a different interpretation. In my experience, those answers come much later sometimes. Give it a damn minute. Be open. Even the seemingly worst scenarios can offer gifts. The woman who started MADD (Mothers Against Drunk Driving) had a son killed by a drunk driver—a tragedy that turned into a national movement bringing profound awareness to the problem and leading to laws being enacted and a major effort in our country to save people from similar tragedies. So:

Let's do our best to stop being shit-magnets.

If shit appears, let's pour whipped cream on that sucker and turn it into something tasty.

Wait it out with faith and a positive mindset. Be open to an answer or a future new path that will give you clarity.

My gifts and clarity came years after my big challenges, and perhaps there is more clarity to come. If you are continually a victim of verbal or physical abuse, unhealthy relationships, health issues, lack of success, take a look at how you might be expecting these things to happen or unconsciously volunteering for them.

Argue for your limitations and, sure enough, they're yours.

- **Richard Bach**

MY FRIEND CAVIN

My friend Cavin Balaster sustained a severe traumatic brain injury. While he was in a coma, his mother was told that Cavin had less than a 10 percent chance of ever regaining consciousness beyond a persistent vegetative state. Cavin didn't walk or talk for months and his left hand was entirely flexed inward. He was breathing and receiving nutrition through a tube, and as you can imagine, a lot went into his recovery after he finally did awake from the coma and regain consciousness. Cavin went on to write a book called *How to Feed a Brain* in which he lays out an easy-to-follow eating style that supplies the brain with the nutrients needed for optimal function. Cavin not only shares his inspiring journey through speaking to audiences and through interviews, but he is also working to improve the standard model of neurorehabilitation. Cavin now works with people who have loved ones in similar situations as they navigate through traumatic brain injuries and other neurological conditions.

Your experience is your experience. I will not tell you that mine was worse or better and I don't even care about comparing the positives and negatives of it. What I can tell you is that you are the hero in this journey and you get to choose your own adventure in this life. You can choose to see parts of your life as terrible and continue to victimize yourself, or you can become your own hero. You are already a hero to someone, so you might as well make that someone, yourself.

- **Cavin Balaster, author of** *How to Feed a Brain* (FeedABrain.com)

CONFIDENT PEOPLE DON'T COMPETE, THEY JUST WIN

When you compete, you lose.

- Elle Russ

How can you win anything if you don't compete? There is a critical nuance worth exploring here. I always compete to win and be the best, but I never compete *against* anyone else. I don't have the mindset of *beating others*, I solely have the mindset of *being the best and winning*. There is a vibrational difference of intention here. Competing against others is, in a way, hoping for another person's failure, and connecting it to your feeling of superiority over them in your success. That is a low self-esteem, low-confidence perspective.

Competing to be the best and winning involves zero negative or comparative energy towards other people. In fact, there is no one else really involved. Sure, the event or competition might have other contestants, but it is your mindset going into the contest that matters. I believe more winning outcomes are tipped in favor of people who adopt the approach of focusing on being the best versus trying to beat someone else.

Some people feel threatened by others who are trying to succeed in the same endeavors, and that fear is precisely the mindset that there is not enough to go around; the fear that someone else might soar higher than you in the same industry or steal your place. That fear generates a feeling of negative competition that in my opinion leads to failure, not success. I always encourage and help others to achieve anything that I currently do myself, because there is enough room for all of us. The more you genuinely encourage and help others succeed at something that you are fearful of being surpassed at, the more you will succeed at that exact endeavor. Wish everyone success while focusing on being the best at whatever you are striving for. What others are doing in the same realm is inconsequential to attaining the successful experiences you desire.

The key lies in understanding that there is infinite abundance available for all of us. There are enormous amounts of wealth, love, happiness, and time just waiting for you. Abundant, happy, successful people are no different from you except that they have a different mindset and outlook. They commit to their plans with the *expectation of success*, yet they are also prepared to change and adjust along the way. Successful people make mistakes too, but unlike others, they use them as positive feedback to educate them and steer them further in the right direction. They do not embody mistakes as overall defeat. Success means different things to different people; all that matters is what *you* want. Is it money? Is it a family? Is it happy friendships? A fulfilling career? All of the above? It is well within your reach, if you set your mind and emotions to the right vibrational station. Success happens when you feel happy and fulfilled, and at ease; it's not about how much stuff you accumulate or how slim you are. There are plenty of fit, wealthy people out there suffering every day from depression, embroiled in contentious relationships, and battling harmful addictions. True, lasting success is based on your peace of mind and how happy you make yourself and others. But no thing or person can generate this power inside of you, only you can do it.

CONFIDENT PEOPLE ARE NOT JEALOUS

To fully appreciate yourself and your life, you have to ignore what others think of you, what others have, and what others do. Only your thoughts influence your happiness

- **Robert Mack,** *Happiness from the Inside Out*

Envy, in a nutshell, is wanting what others have. Jealousy encompasses feelings of insecurity, fear, and envy over lack of possessions, status, or something of personal value. Both involve comparisons, which reflect feelings of insufficiency. Adding to this soup of negative emotions is a sense of injustice that the envied person's advantage is undeserved. And boy, that is a very slippery slope. This combination of inferiority, frustration, and resentment can lead to hostility and passive-aggressive behaviors.

Overcoming envy and jealousy begins with awareness, allowing you to see that the projected stories in your mind are not true, and more importantly are self-defeating. Jealousy can ruin your peace of mind, relationships, and move success further away from you (and besides, no one wants to hang out with a jealous person). Rather than letting jealousy infect your life, soul, and career, use its emergence as a tool to better understand yourself. Envy and jealousy is essentially hoping for the failure of another person. Wishing or hoping that people fail is an irrefutable way to invite that sentiment right back onto you. What you project, you will get.

I have noticed throughout my life that jealous, envious people are not only unhappy, but they often fail, and even if they succeed at attaining the things they sought, the jealousy and unhappiness continued somewhere else in their life. Just like physical health, you have to get to the root of the problem in order to fix it, and the main roots of jealousy and envy are low self-esteem and lack of confidence, along with a feeling of scarcity, as if there is not enough to go around. Do the self-examination and work required so that you can gain the confidence you desire while working towards becoming inspired by (and happy about) the accomplishments of others, rather than turning someone else's gains into manufactured threats against yourself.

If someone contacts me because they want to be in the same

professions as I am, I help them succeed—because aside from never being jealous or envious of another, I don't believe in lack of abundance. There *is* enough to go around. I am awesome, you are awesome, it's all good. We all have our place.

CONFIDENT WOMEN ARE PRO-WOMEN

I refuse to hang out or develop close friendships with women who I sense are unsupportive, gossipy, or jealous. We need a new public relations agent, and I am volunteering for it right now, because the stereotypical competitive discord between women that is reflected on TV and in films, reality shows, and life in general is bullshit. If you are a woman and you have girlfriends who you think are jealous or unsupportive of you—maybe they are! You have to ditch those downers because their negative energy will hold you back and continually challenge your confidence. Besides, if they are jealous, they are secretly hoping you fail, which is a major downer. Bye Felicias.

I love myself too much to hang out with someone who I suspect is jealous and envious. I want you to love yourself too. Start developing friendships with confident women who possess high self-esteem. These women, like me, are in your favor. We got you! We do not compete, we do not get jealous, and we are always rooting for you to prevail. Ladies, get your shit together when it comes to other women so we can encourage each other and build up our self-esteem collectively. Women have had enough challenges fighting oppression throughout history, we don't any need more of that from our own kind. We need to change this dynamic between women and it starts with you, lady.

CONFIDENT PEOPLE TELL IT LIKE IT IS

This topic comes up often in coaching. You know those people everyone feels sorry for? Those people who are seemingly always being taken advantage of in life while everyone says, "Oh poor Joe, you know what his problem is…he's just too nice."

Nope, Joe is not too nice; Joe is a people-pleaser who cannot speak up for himself. People-pleasers have low self-esteem and often go along with situations and say what they think other people want to hear because they want people to like them. They fear rejection. They usually have covert agendas that slowly sink into hidden resentments. You know what people pleasing really is? It's straight up lying. People-pleasers are liars. Confident people with high self-esteem feel no need to bullshit people into liking them, or bullshit people at all. When you lie about your life, your opinions, your feelings, and your desires—when all you have put forth to the world is a manufactured, false version of you—how can you expect anyone to love and respect you?

I Interviewed Dr. Robert A. Glover twice on The Primal Blueprint Podcast (episodes #322 and #367). He is the author of *No More Mr. Nice Guy* and *Dating Essentials for Men.* Dr. Glover is one of my favorite speakers on the topic of "nice guys" or people-pleasers. There are a lot of "nice guys" and "nice girls" out there, and they all have the same qualities and characteristics.

Excerpt from No More Mr. Nice Guy: A Proven Plan for Getting What You Want in Love, Sex, and Life - by Dr. Robert A. Glover

"Nice Guys all believe that if they are "good" and do everything "right" they will be loved, get their needs met, and have a problem-free life. This attempt to be good typically involves trying to eliminate or hide certain things about themselves (their mistakes, needs, emotions), and become what they believe others want them to be (generous, helpful, peaceful) etc.

The nice guy is everywhere:

* He is the relative who lets his wife run the show.

* He is the buddy he will do anything for anybody, but his own life seems to be in shambles.

* He's the guy who frustrates his wife or girlfriend because he is so afraid of conflict but nothing ever gets resolved.

* He is the boss who tells one person what they want to hear, then reserves himself to please someone else.

* He is the man who lets people walk all over him because he doesn't want to rock the boat.

* He's the dependable guy at church or the club who will never say no and would never tell anyone if they were imposing on him.

* He is the man whose life seems so under control until boom, one day he does something to destroy it.

Characteristics of Nice Guys

* Nice guys fix and care take.

* Nice guys seek approval from others.

* Nice guys avoid conflict.

* Nice guys believe they must hide their perceived flaws and mistakes.

* Nice guys seek the right way to do things.

* Nice guys repress their feelings.

* Nice guys often try to be different from their fathers.

* Nice guys are often more comfortable relating to women than men.

* Nice guys have difficulty making their needs a priority.

* Nice guys are manipulative.

* Nice guys are controlling.

* Nice guys give to get.

* Nice guys are passive aggressive.

* Nice guys are full of rage.

* Nice guys are addictive.

* Nice guys have difficulty setting boundaries.

People-pleasers collect resentments, a result of the false communications they put forth. Enough. Step up; speak up. Be authentic with yourself and watch the love, respect, and amazing relationships pour in. Confident people are authentic. Authenticity reigns supreme. People are drawn to and trust others who are authentic with their words and actions, and who say what they mean and mean what they say.

CONFIDENT PEOPLE DON'T JUSTIFY AND APOLOGIZE

Here is a common scenario: Joe asks Bob if he wants to go to a party on Saturday night and Bob goes through a laundry list of justifications and reasons as to why he can't go or doesn't want to; some of them may even be untrue. Maybe Bob just doesn't feel like it but because he's not confident, and he thinks a simple, "No thanks" is not enough of response—as if something more legitimate needs to be the reason for not attending a party. I challenge you to stop yourself the moment you start over-explaining or justifying a position you take on anything. When someone asks me to do something I don't want to do, I just respond with, "Thank you, but I am not available," or "No thanks, but I appreciate the invitation!"

Sometimes my answer is just factual, "I would love to, but I am out of town. Thank you for thinking of me." Of course, some things might require a more in-depth explanation, but for the most part, we over-justify rampantly and unnecessarily.

How many times a day are you apologizing for things that have nothing to do with you? When did this trend start? Stop saying you are sorry when you are not to blame. Stop justifying your declining of invites. People will respect you more because they know you aren't bullshitting them and they will accept your "No, thanks," much more than a weak-ass excuse about why you can't or don't want to accept the invite. Stand your ground and simply say, "No."

Let's be clear: this is not about being heartless and never doing anything you don't want to do. For example, no one really *wants* to help a friend retrieve her car from a tow lot, but you *do actually want do it because you like being a good friend* and helping people you care about. There's a difference between speaking up against what you really do not want versus doing a thing no one really wants to do, but doing it anyway because it is a nice gesture and a lovely thing to help a friend. Wanting to help a friend outweighs wanting to do the thing that you are helping your friend with.

CONFIDENT PEOPLE CHOOSE BATTLES WISELY

Sometimes it's easier and more peaceful to let another person think that they are right. *Confident As Fu*k* people are okay with allowing that to happen, because arguing a point for hours on end is a fool's game for a confident person. Don't be the fool. Choose your battles wisely. When you develop true, refined confidence, you make better choices about what battles you choose to fight with people, because you do not care about being right. I mean, if you know you are right, enjoy that win privately and move on. The moment you start to justify and feel like you have to adamantly prove yourself to another, you just lost the confidence game.

A spiritual guru might say that secretly enjoying that you are right is falling victim to negative aspects of the ego. While our egos can be the culprit in a lot of our messy emotions, actions, and reactions, the ego is not something to be completely destroyed or banished as an imperfection. Many self-help teachers have made the ego your enemy, often associating it with being arrogant or imbecilic. Your ego is not the main culprit in every chaotic affair, your illusion of the self is. You need your ego to arbitrate between unconscious and conscious thoughts and emotions. The ultimate game of life appears to be happiness, whatever that means to you, however you feel it and experience it. You know when you feel fulfilled and happy in life and when you don't. The ego is not going away, so enjoy it for its positive attributes and manage it when it steers you towards negative circumstances.

I think the ego gets a bad rap, and I believe that it is harmless to occasionally allow your ego a few wins. They might be philosophically ill-perceived victories, but they still *feel* like victories. I believe these silent victories fuel our confidence. Throw your ego a bone every now and then. I believe self-preservation in body and ego is inherently primal and I am happy to indulge it on occasion. Being a dominant force can increase self-esteem and self-confidence, and maybe even save your life.

Some people might think I have been rough on strangers who have tried to bully me. This is how I roll: if you are a complete stranger and yell at me and bully me, I will engage my primal instincts to protect myself. There are three strangers in the past five years who have experienced this and instantly regretted it. With those incidents, I have not for one second regretted standing my ground and confronting my bullies. In fact, to this day whenever I think about those incidents, I am so proud of my *Confident As Fu*k* self. These moments in standing up to bullies has fueled my sense of self-worth, self-esteem, and self-confidence. If you think about it from an ancestral perspective, the most capable, dominant ancestors likely prevailed and won favor among the group, because it was a daily game of survival and you needed to be valued by the tribe. You needed to be counted on. And even in our modern day, no one counts on the person who cowers in the face of dominance or danger. When you were in a school athletic scenario and you chose your team, did you choose the least capable? Not a chance. You picked the most confident players for a better chance at winning. Primal skills such as defending ourselves, standing our ground, and speaking up should not be fully suppressed by modern spiritual teachings.

People who claim spiritual superiority might say that the key to life is to never allow yourself to be affected by negative things: just smile, breathe, and move on. Or they might declare that being evolved and spiritual is about achieving a constant state of peace of mind. That might be applicable if I lived on a hippie commune, but I live out here in the real world and that isn't real life, and it's not realistic human behavior. If the ego was completely gone, there would be no more contrasts in life to help propel us forward. There is a fine line between being spiritual and evolved, and not allowing your self-esteem to accept a blast from a cannon. Sometimes you just have to put a bully in their place! It feels good to speak up for yourself. When I wrote and performed sketch comedy for many years in Hollywood, there were only two castmates who embodied the definition of "mean girls." I thought they were both good comedic actors, and I was always supportive of them and genuinely complimented them after performances. I was encouraging and supportive of everyone at the theater, because as I stated, I don't compete against others. Still, I could tell these women wanted nothing to do with me. One of the girls, Liz, always threw me mean glances. I would walk into rehearsal and greet her with a simple, "Hey Liz," and she would roll her eyes and huff away like a fifth grader. I never had interactions with her to give her any reason to dislike me, so I was dumbfounded. Either way, her attitude sucked and was unpleasant to experience, especially since we were all together for the sake of comedy, laughter, and happiness.

I called Liz one evening and this was our conversation:

ELLE (very friendly): "Hey Liz, it's Elle. So, it's obvious that you have some kind of issue with me, but here's the thing: we are working together in a tight-knit group rehearsing and performing *comedy* and all I am asking for is that we be pleasant and courteous to each other. The attitude and glances you are throwing my way on a regular basis are unprofessional. All I ask is that you extend some general professional courtesy my way."

LIZ (in a patronizing tone): "You know what Elle, not everyone is going to like you. I don't think you're funny and for Christ's sake, it's not like we have to be best friends."

ELLE: "Yo Liz, don't flatter yourself thinking I want to be your friend and invite you over for a slumber party, because I definitely don't. I don't give a shit whether you like me or my comedy because I know I'm hilarious and everyone else does too. Your opinion of me 'aint gonna change that. The bottom line is, you are being unprofessional and you know it. If you want to continue this grade school charade, go ahead. I tried." Click.

Here's what happened. In the next 16 weeks that followed, I was the only woman in the group who had sketches chosen for every single show of the season. My comedy was on fire. Some of my best work was written and performed during that time, and I later won awards for it. What other gifts and confirmations did the universe bring me for standing up for myself to a shit storm of mean-girl bullying? Several.

At the next pitch session (where we pitch our sketches to a director in hopes they will be chosen for a show) I pitched some stuff that had everyone cracking up. Liz called me that night after the pitch session and left a very sincere voicemail telling me how brilliant my sketches were and how much I made her laugh. And it gets better! Liz's mean-girl friend had to tuck her tail between her legs when her boyfriend attended one of our shows and insisted that he be introduced to me afterwards because my sketch was his favorite. One night after a show, Liz offered to buy me a drink at the bar next to the theater and we had a pleasant time getting to know each other. I gathered this was her way of apologizing without explicitly apologizing. Unfortunately, Liz continued to be rude to others (but never again to me) and she was reprimanded by the owner of the theater and our director and informed that she would be kicked out of the theater if her behavior continued. Liz quit soon after that.

In my experience, when you stand up to a bully, you always win. I feel like it's the universe rewarding you for loving and honoring your self-esteem. This should go without saying, but if you sense you are in physical danger when confronted with a bully, don't speak up unless you are okay with enduring those consequences. I would choose to have my self-esteem punched versus my face.

CONFIDENCE AND RELIGION:
GET YOUR FAITH IN ORDER

"If you want confidence, then understand how much you matter to God. If God loves you, who cares what anybody else thinks."

– Rick Warren

Confident people with high self-esteem have faith. Not necessarily religious faith in a god; I, for example, am not religious. Confident people have faith in general: faith in themselves, faith in their abilities, faith in the ability to prevail in this lifetime, and of course there are confident people who believe in a god. The foundation of most religions is having faith in the unknown and the unseen: an unknown or unseen entity who loves you, watches over you, and is always by your side helping you through trials and tribulations and celebrations in unpredictable, mysterious ways.

I have faith in universal laws, quantum mechanics, and a sense of faith in a general energy I refer to as "the Universe," and I choose to believe that the Universe is always working in my favor. Even when bad shit happens I have faith that there will be a prize for me at the end. My faith is not too far off from a religious person who might believe in the biblical God. Call it God, the universe, Allah; it doesn't really matter because faith is faith.

True faith is having a sense of confidence connected to you feeling accepted by god, and that your future is secure because god is watching over you. It is illogical to declare faith in a god but have no confidence in yourself, because that means you do not actually have faith in god. If you declare faith in a god, then it must follow based on what every religion teaches about god, that you should have faith in yourself. Faith in your ability to learn, to change, to grow, to be happy. Remember, god loves you even when you screw up, right? You can always ask for forgiveness. You can always do better. Use god and your religion to the advantage it inherently offers you.

Stop sauntering around on a religious high-horse declaring your spirituality and devotion to god unless you are tooting your own horn the same way your god would! If god *always* has faith in you, why would you not have faith in yourself? It makes no sense if you think about it. Use your religion to build self-esteem. I have spoken to so many people who are in a state of fear and negativity for many years and yet continue to go to church and claim to have faith in their god. Sure, it might feel good to their ego and it might check a box of ego-spirituality: "Look everyone in my town and community, I am such a faithful churchgoer! I am a good Christian!" That is just false religious pontification, and we all know those people. Forget going to church if you are not going to show up for your god and embrace the tenants of what churches and religion represent. You have to step up and start to see yourself the way your god does: perfect as you are right now, and instilled with god's faith in you. You are perfect and also forgivable in times of lack of integrity.

People who claim to be religious yet lack self-esteem and confidence must resolve these contradictions. You must move forward in developing faith in yourself, and that will strengthen your relationship to your god, and vice-versa. This applies to whatever religious being, prophet, or ethereal energy you believe in. Go out there and get your religious confidence back.

CON(FIDENCE) ARTISTS: THE MISUSE OF CONFIDENCE

Con artists lie, cheat, and steal, and they employ the tactic of using confidence to manipulate their targets. They are often very perceptive, great actors, charming and adept at preying upon others. Confident people are trusted, and the con artist knows this.

They convince a target to trust them prior to manipulation. They are confident in their abilities to fool a person, so that confidence is real. However, like a lot of projections of false confidence, they can get busted. They feel that they are immune to getting caught, which leads to their downfall. It may take two weeks or 20 years, but it catches up eventually even if they don't get caught. You can manipulate people with confidence and misuse it, but you cannot escape the deep lack of integrity and loneliness in such behaviors.

CONFIDENCE WON'T OVERRIDE IGNORANCE OR LACK OF PREPARATION

One of the Hollywood industry fails I witnessed speaks to this point. Two major award-winning film producers approached me and my sitcom-writing partner about assisting them with their first comedy endeavor. They appeared to have major false confidence about their "brilliant" idea for a sitcom. They were not writers by nature or trade, they were just successful film producers—but like a lot of people in Hollywood, they thought it was going to be easy to become a writer and bust out a successful sitcom.

They wrote a half-ass sitcom pilot and presented us with another 30 pages of character notes and descriptions of show scenarios—none of them funny. They felt they had already done all of the major legwork and the only thing needed was to hire a couple of talented writers to shape up their already-existing sitcom script. Here was their brilliant idea: the sitcom would take place in a veterinarian's office, and the comedy would ensue based on all of the whacky characters they created—and because animals are so cute and funny. That would be an extra desirable comedy element.

My writing partner and I read their materials and shook our heads in disbelief. It was one of those so-bad-it-was-good amateur first attempts, violating all tenants of comedy writing. We know, because we had been there ourselves once; we can clearly see the classic mistakes and pitfalls of a newbie. After reading the pilot, the first thing I did was search the Internet to see if anyone else had done a similar TV show. What did I find? Just the year prior, a TV show that took place in a veterinarian's office was canceled from a major network, mainly because PETA (People for the Ethical Treatment of Animals) had received thousands of signatures and protested the network. PETA's issue with the show was that they did not believe animals should "work" regardless of caring and kind conditions given to them; they were opposed to animals working, period. They had signed petitions and protested the show, and the network canceled it.

These people were major award-winning producers whom you would assume might have done their research before spending hours developing a sitcom. Instead, they wasted a lot of time and creative effort. It took one Internet search to immediately blow up their entire project. It was un-sellable before they even started. No network was going to entertain such a project based on what transpired the year before.

You can have confidence, be motivated, and take action, but that cannot override ignorance and lack of preparation. Do your research first. Also, if you think you have funny ideas and feel like you are a great judge of comedy, think again. You need other skills to be an effective comedy writer—like understanding the formula for writing a successful sitcom, for starters. No sitcom you have ever seen is funny because of the location. It is always about the relationships and scenarios between the characters. Comedy does not ensue because it takes place in a doctor's office or a bar, comedy happens within situations and relationship foibles that the characters find themselves caught up in. And now you know: it is not a bright idea to write a TV show that takes place in a veterinarian's office because PETA will be all over your ass.

PART 3

CONFIDENCE CHRONICLES

URBAN LEGEND OR NOT, IT'S STILL AWESOME

One of my favorite urban legends about self-esteem and confidence supposedly comes from a college application more than 25 years ago. Legend has it that the essay portion of the student applications that year prompted applicants to steer their essays in response to the following directive: "Define Courage." Supposedly, one applicant submitted an essay with just *one word:*

This.

Take a moment with that. Just one word: "This." It's genius on so many levels. It instantaneously defines courage in a multitude of ways. What massive courage this applicant had in order to restrain from elaborating or using up space on the application (which most would assume was what the college expected). The courage and intelligence to comprehensively define a thing with one damn word—you cannot get more efficient than using one word to capture your thoughts.

This applicant, with just one word, displayed their level of intelligence, humor, and philosophical tendencies. That applicant was courageous and *Confident As Fu*k!*

FROM SUICIDAL TO CONFIDENT

Shyness has a strange element of narcissism, a belief that how we look, how we perform, is truly important to other people.

- Andre Dubus

The most extreme example of a person who went from ground zero with self-esteem and confidence to a happy, confident person with self-esteem is a client of mine we'll call Tracy. Tracy is 53 years old and still working on course-correcting destructive childhood patterns. She was raised by emotionally distant parents and was crippled with shyness as a child. Her parents sent her to a psychologist at the age of seven because they didn't know what to do with their socially awkward child. Tracy was in therapy for more than 30 years.

After Tracey's mother died, her father pitted Tracy and her brother against each other, often using money or material things as bait, playing favorites deliberately and creating turmoil between the siblings—something they finally resolved in their late 40s. In her formative years, Tracy didn't receive unconditional love from her parents and to make matters worse, her therapist was *paid to care about her*, so there was a perception in Tracy's mind regarding the exchange of money connected with someone paying attention to you. She felt her parents were paying someone else to love her because they could not. Tracy grew up not trusting her parents, or anyone else. She was bullied at school and unfortunately assaulted by a gang of fellow students. This trauma continued to affect her life and all of her relationships.

Tracy was crippled with shyness, didn't trust anyone, and had extremely low self-esteem and zero confidence in herself. She ultimately evolved into one of the biggest people-pleasers and co-dependents you have ever seen. She would try to buy friendship or love (and then not trust it, because how could you trust something you paid for that didn't come naturally? Destructive pattern, check!). She would continually repeat and replay what was familiar to her in childhood, and it would go something like this: "See, you can't trust anyone because no one loves me unconditionally; there is always an angle." She would lie about stuff just to get you to like her (classic people-pleasing behavior) which would, of course, backfire because when the person would like her, she knew deep inside that they liked a false version of herself. How could anyone love the *real* Tracy when she only showed a manufactured, fake-ass version? Around and round she went, "Ah ha! See, you can't trust anyone!" She was always proving her past traumas right.

Tracy ultimately experienced unconditional love when she became pregnant and gave birth to her daughter. The casual boyfriend was a closet drug addict (a perfect boyfriend choice for a codependent people-pleaser) so Tracy had to step up and become a single mom. It was actually the best gift she could have received. Her unhealthy codependent *relationship based on lies* with her daughter's father led her to finally receiving and giving unconditional love. She became the sole parent with full custody for the first seven years of her daughter's life. No perceived competition from a co-parent, no ill-perceived projections of her daughter playing favorites between father and mother. Her daughter loves and worships her, and Tracy finally felt and understood unconditional love.

Tracy hit rock bottom when her people-pleasing, lying, and truckload of insecurities led her to a codependent relationship, which led to a pregnancy she never intended. But her daughter is the best thing that ever happened for her spiritual growth, and in the process of raising a child, Tracy has come to see more and more the tragedy that was her childhood. The glaring contrast between the love she feels for her daughter compared to her destructive childhood experiences has led to a beautiful love between a mother and daughter and increased healing for her past wounds. It took a while, but she achieved new, healthy patterns. She no longer lies to people to get them to like her. She stands up for herself. She was suicidal for a long time, and is now happy with no hidden desires to kill herself.

Tracy was born rich and never had to work a day in her life if she didn't feel like it. She is worth millions and millions of dollars. So, if you think winning the lottery is going to change your self-esteem or make you confident or happy, know that it won't. Money cannot override what you feel inside about yourself. Money will only make it worse. Money sometimes cannot buy successful therapy either. In Tracy's case, money led to years of indulging in five-star restaurants, expensive clothes, cars, shoes, and stuff. Money never solved a damn thing for Tracy except as a way to foster codependent relationships and rescue men who were financially struggling, so she could have some power over them (exactly as her father did with Tracy and her brother). Money just deepened her problems.

All of the decades of therapy is not what turned it around for her. Tracy's ultimate success in building self-esteem and confidence mostly came from within, through self-examination and reading books on happiness, codependency, addiction, people-pleasing, and other topics in self-improvement. She finally did the work. Of all things, what truly turned her life around was the audiobook *The Secret* and several audiobooks by author Dr. Wayne Dyer. She immersed herself in audiobooks on the subjects of the power of intention and creating your own reality. In all of those years of therapy, she would just sit there receiving comfort from therapists who would agree with her that her parents were to blame for her current state of affairs. Therapy for Tracy was often destructive, because she would leave a session even angrier and in a deeper sense of blame and victimhood, thinking, "See! Told ya so! Yet another psychology professional has just confirmed that my parents are the reason that this is why I am the way I am!" Thousands and thousands of dollars were spent on a variety of therapists and it turns out a few $20 audiobooks took Tracy from suicidal thoughts and self-sabotage to self-reflection and success.

Tracy understands now that *she allowed her childhood to generate her adult reality.* She now generates her reality from her newfound confidence and from a place of self-worth and self-compassion. Tracy *parents herself* now instead of waiting for her 87-year-old father to someday meet her parenting expectations. She would tell you today that she has moments where old fears creep in or she occasionally gets triggered by something her father does (her father still attempts to pit the siblings against each other), except Tracy doesn't fall for it anymore. She sees it for what it is. Instead of fearfully jumping in to participate and engage in this destructive pattern, she disengages. She stopped sharing exciting and important things in her life with her father, because Tracy learned how to not let him be a downer in her life.

HOW YOU WALK INTO A PLACE

> *"I taught myself confidence. When I'd walk into a room and feel scared to death, I'd tell myself, 'I'm not afraid of anybody.' And people believed me. You've got to teach yourself to take over the world."*
>
> – **Priyanka Chopra**

Laura is a lovely aesthetician from whom I get facials, and she was in need of self-esteem and self-confidence. One day during a facial she said, "You know, I was thinking about you recently, because I was thinking about how when I walk into a crowded restaurant or public place, I feel insecure and self-conscious. I thought, 'I bet Elle never feels this way' and so I'm wondering, how do you feel when you walk into a place?" Without hesitation I said, "I walk into every single place like I own that motherfucker." She laughed, "I thought so."

My statement to Laura sounds cocky as hell, right? Who says stuff like that? I do. Because it is true. Let me explain further: I don't walk into a room full of people feeling like I am superior to them, or feeling like I am going to impress them, or feeling like I need to talk at all. I walk into a place with an overall sense of curiosity and openness to learn or maybe have a new conversation or experience. I have no agenda and not a care in the world about what others in that place think of me, my outfit, my body, or my accomplishments. I am comfortable with myself in a room full of strangers. If you can reach a place of ease when alone in a crowd, it is an incredibly comforting, confident feeling.

A life-hack on this is to force yourself to go out alone and have a meal at a crowded restaurant, and just people-watch while affirming to yourself, "I don't care what anyone in here thinks of me, I am here to observe them and I am practicing being alone in a crowd." It can feel awkward and weird, but when you leave the restaurant you will have a newfound sense of confidence, realizing it wasn't as bad as you thought. You will be proud of yourself. Going to a restaurant alone might not be as fun as going with a friend, but it is a great exercise in building confidence.

BASKETBALL CONFIDENCE: THIS WHITE GIRL CAN JUMP

You must expect great things of yourself before you can do them.

– **Michael Jordan**

Confidence in sports can also be a form of dominance. Fake-outs, name calling—there are lots of different tactics employed to psych out an opponent with the goal of rendering your competition weak or afraid. If you engage in athletic competitions, you must develop some sports confidence and be prepared for dominant personalities attempting to trip you up. My confidence in sports was tested when I was kicked out of a Jesuit high school (the many little reasons why this happened don't really matter; I was caught smoking in the girl's restroom, failed a few classes, and found myself in two "Breakfast Club" Saturday detention scenarios) and sent to another school. The majority of students at the new school were black kids from a neighborhood called Cabrini Green, a housing project known for its high crime rate. (Cabrini Green has since been torn down.)

As a white student at the school, I learned the ground rules from other students. You never had a locker on the second or third floor, and you tried to avoid spending any more time than needed on those floors, or in the basement of the school for fear of either having something stolen, getting your ass kicked because you were a white kid, or getting mixed up in a fight that was inevitably going to start around you. As a result, all of the white kids had lockers on the first floor, close to the Principal's office and the outdoor exits. One student told me: "Listen, when these girls leave the lunch-room, they will walk down the first-floor hallway and smack your back or pull your hair, and you just have to suck it up, and don't say a word or you will get your ass beat." Welcome to Lincoln Park High School. One weekend, a beloved and talented black student who was active in the school's theater and dance department was accidentally shot during a gun fight between a Puerto Rican gang and a black gang. The following Monday at school, black gang members threw a couple of Puerto Rican kids out of the school windows and started various fights with Puerto Rican students. It was a pretty horrendous environment—students were in and out of jail constantly, we had a police officer on campus, and the teenage pregnancy rate was disheartening. Many students dropped out after their sophomore year since the law didn't require them to continue on after the age of 16; a freshman class might start out with 900 students, but the graduating class was about 200.

I love basketball and have played ever since I was about seven years old. I really missed the sport because I had not played for a couple of years. I decided to try out for the basketball team. All interested players were told to meet in a classroom and wait for the coaches to arrive before putting our gym clothes on and heading to the gym. I arrived early and sat in the empty classroom. Minute after minute, the room began to fill up with fellow students, all black girls from Cabrini Green. One girl looked at me and laughed with the other girls, "Check out this white bitch. She thinks she can play ball." Another followed up with, "Cracker-ass bitch, you 'aint shit." I was instantly humiliated and unprepared for these attacks. I was the only white girl trying out for the Varsity team—it was 20 tough-as-hell black girls from the projects, and me, a five-foot-two-inch short, white, blond, blue-eyed cracker. What these girls didn't know is that competition fuels my confidence and enhances my athletic abilities. These girls mocked me and my attempt to make the team. They were falsely confident in their assumption that because I was white, there was no way my skills in basketball could trump theirs. All I kept thinking to myself were thoughts like, "Nope. Not today. Don't you dare let these girls fuck up your game, you are going to go into that gym and kick some ass. You *have* to do this, you cannot bail and you cannot be the white girl who sucks at basketball today. Not today, motherfuckers." I couldn't speak up for myself, because they would have beaten the crap out of me, so I let my actions do the talking.For the entire tryouts, I was on fire, but the ultimate moment of basketball glory came when we were each challenged to an "around the world," an attempt at making five three-point baskets in a row from outside the three-point arc line of the court. Never in my life had I sunk more than two baskets in a row on such a challenge, but I was fired up with extra competition-confidence that day. I made every single one of those baskets. No girl in the gymnasium came close. To this day, I have never repeated it. And I continued to bask in that glory throughout the year, because our team was undefeated.

I hope one day to reconnect with my former teammates Barbara and Tina; I have tried to locate them over the years. These girls looked out for me when we traveled to other schools that were more crime-ridden than our school. They watched my back at away games, and a few times Barbara drove me home or made sure I got to the El train safely. One time Barbara hustled me out of another high school because some of our teammates were about to fight the losing team players in the locker room. "Get your ass to the train right now, shit is about to go down." It was very stressful. I was the only white girl at most of our away games—and I mean *the only white girl in the entire gymnasium.* The stands were filled with black kids yelling out "cracker" and "white devil" or "white bitch" or "honkey ass bitch" as I played against their team. It was the most intense sports pressure I have ever been under, to focus on playing a sport that I love while at the same time having racial slurs screamed at me by people in the stands and also by my opponents on the court directly to my face as I dribbled the ball. At 5'2" I was always significantly shorter than everyone on both teams, which is of course physically intimidating. Because I was so much shorter than every player and could not shoot a basket over these tall women, I gained the skills of setting up the plays, running the full court for lay-ups, and mastering three-pointers. To this day, I have a killer three-point shot. Aside from that, my time on that basketball team with Barbara and Tina was one of the greatest experiences I have had, and hands down one of the best confidence enhancers of my life.

> *To be a great champion you must believe you are the best. If you're not, pretend you are.*
>
> – **Muhammed Ali**

FIRST IMPRESSIONS

I have been interviewed numerous times over the years. One time an interviewer said to me, "I will record your introduction after the interview and I'll splice it into the audio later" (A common practice). When I heard the introduction after the interview was released, I busted out laughing. He said, "Elle Russ is a spitfire. She is someone I would really love to work with, but I wouldn't want to mess with." Through my laughter, I thought "Exactly, I am so glad he got the right impression." What can I say, I'm *Confident As Fu*k*.

When you are a no-BS, authentic human being who is honest with your words and actions, people respect your opinions more than those who blow smoke. My castmates at the comedy theater knew this about me. One time after I watched a sketch show at our theater, I profusely complimented the director. He said to me, "That really means a lot coming from you Elle, because I know you don't bullshit people." If I go out of my way to compliment you on a talent or a way of thinking or anything, it's truly how I feel. The same thing happened with a fellow author. I gave them a very complimentary, personal review of their book and received a similar response: "That means a lot coming from you Elle, because I know you don't blow smoke."

I am so glad that these are the impressions I make, because they also increase my level of self-esteem every time someone recognizes and appreciates my authenticity. You always know where you stand with me. Isn't that preferable to walking on eggshells? Isn't it preferable to know that a friend is always honest with you? Start being authentic with your words and actions and you will attract more of those types of people into your life. When you are always authentic, you are trusted more by people and your opinions will be more valued over the opinions of others—and that alone has advantages in the workplace in all types of situations.

CONFIDENCE IN DECLARING YOUR WORTH

You get in life what you have the courage to ask for.

– **Oprah Winfrey**

I had to put my confidence to the test momentarily when I was pitching my first book to *New York Times* Bestselling author (and ultimately the publisher of my first book) Mark Sisson. We were brainstorming about possibilities for *The Paleo Thyroid Solution*. Mark and I were sitting in his house just spit-balling ideas, and he proposed something valid in terms of strategy. The subject of my book was medical in nature, and I possess a degree in philosophy, not medicine. So he suggested, "Elle, what if you share writing credit on the book cover with a doctor even though you will write the book and they will not get any profits—it would give you more credibility." It wasn't a bad idea; many people do this. My response—which was immediate—was probably one of the most confident responses that has ever come out of my mouth.

My response was, "Mark, I am a woman writer. Do you have any idea how many glass ceilings I have had to break to get here? I am not going to share writing credit with a doctor who didn't write one word of this book. If I am writing it, I want sole writing credit." Mark instantly responded with an, "Okay yep, I get it." And we moved on in our discussion. That was that. A simple declaration and no argument from him. The whole discussion lasted ten seconds and had no tension or negativity about it. Also, Mark Sisson is *Confident As Fu*k* too, so nothing about my counterpoint or disagreeing with the idea would have bothered him anyway.

A lot of writers in that situation might have acquiesced to the publisher—especially if they had never written a book before. Here I am with a badass, multi-millionaire businessman whom I not only admire, love, and respect, but who held the power to manifest my publishing dreams. I could have remained silent and gone along with his suggestion for fear of what he would think of me, or afraid that my response would kill the deal. I am so happy that I did not agree to it, because I would have regretted it to this day. Most men don't think about what it's like for women to work in a male-dominated industry, and sometimes you have to point it out to them, that's all; they just live in a different world. Mark is one of the most pro-women men I have ever met, and he understood instantly.

CONFIDENCE CAN BE SILENT

People mistakenly conclude that confidence is only about an outward display or public performance, like being the most gregarious, charming guy at the party. Some of the most confident people I know are the quietest people in the room. One of my best friends is just such a confident person; he may not speak much at all. In fact, you may see him standing alone in a corner, and some people would incorrectly assume that he is uncomfortable or might think, "Look at that poor guy over there in the corner all alone." But the truth is, he is just standing there comfortably by himself observing the rest of the party. That is confidence too.

Performance-based confidence, like speaking to a room full of people, can be acquired and learned. Some people are natural performers, and other people need to cultivate it. You can have outward confidence and be the most insecure, non-confident person on the inside with low self-esteem. Ideally, you want to cultivate both. You want to be *Confident As Fu*k*. Being confident is not the same thing as being cocky. I am absolutely comfortable in touting my abilities and I will declare my strengths. However, cockiness usually has an air of insecurity behind it because if you have the desire to try to out-shine or boast or brag to people, ultimately you're just trying to convince them that you are confident through a dominating persona. Truly confident people don't need to convince others of it. They declare their worth and move on. If you don't see it, they don't care.

WHEN NOT SPEAKING UP (OR EVEN LYING) IS A GOOD CALL

If I am invited to a friend's grandmother's house for dinner and she is 95 years old and, let's say, utters a homophobic slur, I am not going to use that moment to try and teach her a lesson about tolerance. She is 95 years old. She's not my grandmother. In those situations, for me, that's not a battle worth fighting. It's someone's Thanksgiving dinner, for crying out loud. Let it go. That is for the family to talk to her about. It is not appropriate to disrupt a dinner and make a scene because I have the need to be right or to try to convince her that LGBT people are not sinners. Sometimes, you just have to pick your battles.

Furthermore, if I am meeting your mother for the first time and she points to her ugly sweater and asks, "What do you think of this cute sweater I just bought!" I will straight up lie to her face by agreeing, "It's really cute, looks great on you." Why? Because otherwise, you are being a downer. She obviously loves the sweater and she's not really looking for an honest opinion, she is looking for me to validate her purchase and her excitement about the damn sweater. I will give it to her. However, if you are one of my friends and you sincerely ask me what I think of your new sweater and it's ugly, I am going to tell you. (Then again, my friends know that I am going to give my brutally honest opinion, so they wouldn't ask me unless they were prepared to hear it.) Some of the greatest compliments I receive from my friends is when they are about to ask my opinion on something and they say, "I am asking you because I know you will tell me the truth." Yes, I will.

PART
4

SHAME
DISABLES
CONFIDENCE

Shame is an unpleasant self-conscious emotion typically associated with a negative evaluation of the self, feelings of distress, exposure, mistrust, powerlessness, worthlessness, and a desire to withdraw from others or society in general. You can be confident with high self-esteem and yet, if there is a deep sense of shame hidden in the background, it will eventually impact your life and self-esteem in unexpected and negative ways.

THE SHAME OF DISABILITY AND THE DISABILITY OF SHAME

I am not happy and successful despite my disability, I am happy and successful because of my disability.

- Elle Russ

The saying, "God laughs when we make plans," has been glaringly true in my life. I have a twenty-year story that could fill an entire book, but I will share the main threads of it here. I have a permanent physical disability. The state of California rated me at a 40 percent disability back in 1998, although you would never know it. You cannot visibly see my impairment and as far as anyone can tell, I look totally "normal."

When I was 21 years old and graduated from college, I just wanted to become a lawyer, get a steady job, make a ton of money, and be financially secure. Based on what I mentioned earlier about my childhood story of not trusting men to support me, becoming an attorney felt like the most secure path to financial freedom, and I was very interested in law. It felt it was my legacy, as my *Confident As Fu*k* grandmother was the youngest practicing attorney in the state of Illinois and was part of the effort to allow women to serve on juries. I felt like a legal career was in my DNA, so after college, I got a salary-with-benefits job as the executive assistant to the owner of a company. I was just passing time, waiting to be accepted into law schools. It turns out, the universe had other plans for me.

I was the 10th person hired at a rapidly growing privately held start-up company during the tech boom of the '90s. The company was growing so fast that I was promoted three months later, and then promoted again two to three months after that, and so on. Before I knew it, I was 22 years old and had my own office with a view, a collection of expensive suits, and was rolling in the dough with an income and bonuses equaling about $10,000 a month, well on my way to making $325,000 yearly. I was the highest-producing employee among ten other co-workers who held the same position, and all of them were 15 years older than me. I staffed and helped manage about 100 computer consultants throughout the state of California on big tech projects at Fortune 500 companies.

I would sit in my office and think to myself, "I am set. This is it. I don't need to go to law school anymore. I am making more than a first-year attorney. Forget law school, I'm going to stay here and I am going to become a part owner of this company someday. By the time I'm 40, I will be able to retire and buy a couple of houses and have a few Porsches in the driveway." I was not overly-confident to have those thoughts, as my career was indeed going in that direction. And life was great. As someone who had been expelled from high school, I felt vindicated that I was more professionally successful at this point than any student who had graduated from both high schools I attended. I felt triumphant over my past failures. Everything was going according to plan—in fact, much faster and better than I had planned.

One evening after work, I asked a friend and co-worker to come over and help me carry a lightweight chair that I had bought from a local store only a block away from my apartment. The chair wasn't heavy but it was too bulky and awkward for me to carry on my own. As we were carrying the chair home, every fifteen seconds I had to ask him to put the chair down because my wrists felt weak. I couldn't hold the chair in my hands for very long. I remember thinking, "Something isn't right here," but I dismissed it.

Within the next week or so, both of my arms and hands became severely inflamed and I was in constant, chronic pain. I could not wipe myself after going to the bathroom without pain, I could not hold a fork in my hand without pain. I could not hold a coffee cup or anything in my hands. I could not even hold my boyfriend's hand without excruciating pain. My arms were dead-weight and useless and felt like they were on fire. I couldn't even gesture with my hands when I spoke. I had to exchange my purse for a backpack because I needed to be completely hands-free as much as possible. I couldn't sleep on my sides anymore, and my arms would go completely numb every night. I was beside myself with pain and depression. My friends had to help me carry groceries home from the store. I ordered take-out often because I could not wash dishes.

I didn't know anything about workplace injuries or worker's compensation, because I was a clueless 22-year-old in her first adult job and I had never been exposed to these things or even knew they existed. A co-worker contacted human resources and told them they were concerned about me because I was complaining about my hands not working right. The human resources manager called me and instructed me to fill out a worker's compensation form. Often when someone files a claim, the employee leaves work and gets paid by worker's comp until they recover and can return to the job. But I was bringing in about two million dollars of revenue for the company, and they needed me—I was too valuable to lose. Eventually I was diagnosed with chronic tendonitis and tenosynovitis in my arms and my hands.

The company I worked for made their best efforts to support me through recovery efforts. I left early for physical therapy appointments three times a week, and could telecommute from home on those days. At one point, they hired a temp to be my hands for me, but I still had to use my hands and arms for dialing the phone and taking notes during interviews of potential hires. I still had to get myself ready for work in the morning and do basic things with my hands, and all of it was too much for my condition. I could not even wipe tears away from my eyes without excruciating pain.

As you read this, you have probably adjusted your hands many times in the past few minutes, perhaps you even wiped your nose or scratched your head and don't even realize how automatic hand use and hand movements are for you. Most people take their hands and arms for granted. So, if your hands and arms are working great right now, please take a moment to be grateful.

I hoped the pain would get better and go away, but the opposite happened. After six months of physical therapy and having a temp substitute for some of my hand-based activities at work, the human resources manager called me in and said, "This is your last day at work here, we have to put you out on workmen's comp. From now on you will be paid through them, and if you recover, we would be happy to have you back." That's it? Just, "Goodbye, sorry!" I was confused, frightened, and in chronic pain. My hands and arms were useless. I was very fearful about my future.

I never had surgery for my condition because it wasn't applicable to my situation, but the first doctor overseeing my disability was one of the best hand surgeons in the world, Dr. Gabriel Kind of the Buncke Clinic in San Francisco. People flew in from all over the world to see him, and I sat next to people in physical therapy who had accidentally sawed off their hands and fingers and had them surgically reattached. One seven-year-old boy had all of the skin ripped off one of his arms in a freak accident. I was also in physical therapy next to dentists who had my condition from repetitively using tiny dental instruments every day, all day. I met a woman who got my condition from uncorking 200 bottles of wine several nights a week at a restaurant.

After a year of physical therapy and six months after being put on workmen's comp and staying at home, not working at all, came one of the hardest days of my entire life. And I am crying right now as I write this, because it still makes me sad for my former self who felt so hopeless in that moment. Dr. Kind said to me, "Unfortunately you are going to have this for the rest of your life and it's probably not going to get better. You will never be able to go back to that job or any job like it where you have to use your hands repetitively."

I lost it; I drowned in despair. At the age of 22, being told that I would never be able to use my hands in the ways most people were able to shattered my soul. Being told I was never going to be able to return to my kickass well-paid job brought me intense fear about my financial future. I went back to my apartment with my useless, dead arms and I sat in front of my window, and the most overwhelming sense of shame took over me. I thought, "What man is ever going to want to marry me? I can't be a wife or a mom; I can barely feed myself. I can't take care of children. I won't be able to even button their clothes in the morning or get them ready for school, much less hold an infant in my arms. I can't even hold a cup in my hand. Who the hell is going to want me? Who is going to want to love and deal with a woman with dead arms?" I looked up to the sky. I didn't believe in god, but I was grasping for something outside of this world to help me. I probably had my first unintentional moment of gratitude, thinking, "Okay, if my arms and hands are not going to work, *at least I have them*. At least I have arms and hands."

In the Spring of 1998, the human resources manager informed me that our company had a great own-occupation long-term disability policy that I should apply for. Policies like this no longer exist unless you bought them more than 20 years ago—they are no longer offered by insurance companies. It was a miracle that my company offered such a policy for their employees, and it was the saving grace of my life. The policy basically states that if you become disabled and can never return to your own occupation, you receive 60 percent of your income until you are 65 years old. The insurance company approved me for benefits and calculated my benefits to be about $45,000 a year.

I was 22 years old and essentially retired on long-term disability. Everyone else I knew was just starting their careers and lives, and mine had abruptly come to an end. Some people thought it was like winning the lottery. I had friends that were like, "Oh man, that's so cool. If I were you, I would travel to Tahiti one week and Paris the next!" But my pre-injury plan was to get rich so that I didn't have to worry about depending on someone else supporting me financially, and then I became instantly dependent on an insurance company to support me. Furthermore, I was mortified and embarrassed about accepting money from something with the word "disability" in it, because we all know how the world feels about hand-outs. Even though it was private insurance not paid for by other people's taxes, as an alpha female with a lot of pride, it was a huge hit to accept my permanent injury and $45,000 a year. In California, that doesn't go very far.

My shame started to increase because of other people's comments and questions about my disability. Once my best friend at the time made a snide remark to the effect of, "Well, you know what, some of us have to work, so..." In tears I responded, "Oh, do you want to trade arms with me? Are you seriously jealous of me because I am disabled and don't have to work? I will trade arms with you right now!" And with comments like that and skeptical questions from people who cannot wrap their head around a condition they cannot visibly see, I started to think, "Maybe it's just better that I shut up and don't say anything to anybody. I don't need the questions or the judgments."

Over the years, I have come to realize that people are much more compassionate and understanding towards a person missing an arm or someone in a wheelchair, because people can see it and therefore understand it. When you have a condition that people cannot see, they ask a ton of questions about it, and I grew weary of going through the entire sensational story over and over again—because it also brought up the emotional pain of having the disability and the fears I had about my future potential. No amount of money was ever going to bring my fucking arms back, so I did not see it the way my twenty-something friends were seeing it. They thought it was cool, but I thought I was fucked.

The chronic pain eventually lessened as I spent more and more time away from work. I did everything I could to help my condition, from acupuncture to hypnosis to regular massage, and I even starting swimming in a pool with a snorkel and a mask so I could kick around in the water without using my arms. As my condition became more tolerable, the shame of my physical disability combined with the shame of being paid by an insurance company disabled me emotionally. This affected me immensely in romantic relationships. I could not bring myself to tell my story to a man I was dating, because I was afraid to be perceived as defective, a liability, and I feared that I would ultimately be rejected—because who wants to be with someone who is already permanently injured for the rest of their life at the age of 22? My reasoning included thoughts like, "Why would a guy choose me when they could just find a non-disabled women who can do so many more things that I cannot? I don't think I would choose to be with a man that couldn't use his arms like me; I wouldn't want that myself." Feelings and emotions of worthlessness, fear, embarrassment, distress, and mistrust overwhelmed me every time I started dating someone.

I falsely concluded that hiding it was safer and better. I thought hiding my shame and hiding my disability would make the shame disappear. I wanted to get away from talking about my disability, so I just didn't talk about it. But that shame created a big secret in my life that I had to hide from people. And this is how it would manifest in friendships or relationships: I cannot get close to you and we cannot be *real friends* because you don't know this big thing about me and my life, so while you may trust me and open up to me and share your life and experiences with me, how can I trust you in return? You don't even really know me for who I truly am, because I have this dark secret in the background that if you found out about, you might reject me, judge me, or be jealous of me.

And so it went on like that, for almost two decades. Aside from my former coworkers and doctors, only a handful of friends and family members knew my disability story. Dealing with my shame is something I really wish I had dealt with sooner, because it was more disabling to my life than the disability itself. I would also rope other people into my shame and put them in awkward positions. For example, when I started dating a guy and they would meet my friends and I would prep them beforehand, "Okay, he doesn't know about my arms, so don't mention anything." There are some guys out there who I dated and I never shared my story with. I was too ashamed. When those relationships would end, I would feel relieved and sort of used it as an excuse, "Well that didn't work out, so I am glad I never said anything to them in the first place."

Really though? Would it have worked out differently had I just had the courage to be vulnerable and be open about my situation? I don't believe in woulda, coulda, shoulda's, and I have not looked back at any man as "the guy that got away," but I learned this lesson to prevent myself from future issues—and hopefully it will encourage you to deal with whatever shame you feel, so that you don't let it control a part of your life for 20 years.

People would say to me, "I don't understand why you are ashamed; it wasn't your fault that you were injured." But it doesn't matter if you have a reason that people think is valid: shame is shame no matter which way you cut it. People have shame about being molested as a child, about their body or their sexuality. It doesn't matter what you're ashamed of, shame disables confidence and self-esteem. It is all the same shitty emotion and it's one of the lowliest emotions a person can have; it rips into your self-esteem and negatively affects your life experiences.

When I received my first monthly long-term disability check I thought, "How am I going to make a life for myself and earn more money than this?" My second thought was, "Well, I still have my voice. Maybe I can somehow use my voice." And just two months later, I began a 20-year journey pursuing a career where I could use my voice instead of my hands and arms. I enrolled in a miniature summer MFA program at the American Conservatory Theater in San Francisco. I figured I would have to become professionally trained in acting, singing, and all things voice-related so I could climb up the ladder in another industry. I took action.

Ever since, I have had the most amazing experiences. From

performing sketch comedy at The Second City - Chicago and ACME Comedy Theater in Hollywood, to interning in Hollywood casting offices and going out for amazing auditions as an actor. I landed an acting role in a movie and later had the pleasure of being hired twice by two of my favorite comedians and comedy producers. I was having fun and dream-come-true experiences, but still nothing was yielding an income that could get me out of my financial dependency on the insurance company, and that was—and is still—my ultimate goal.

Five years into my acting and voice journey, I was side-swiped with another physical ailment, severe hypothyroidism. As you might imagine, my first thought was, "You have to be fucking kidding me! This cannot be happening! Why me?" I was debilitated with that disease and suffered for the majority my 30's with two bouts of severe hypothyroidism. About six years of my life was lost to hypothyroidism and the severe symptoms that came with it.

Fortunately, the disability policy from my hand injury allowed me to stay at home, rest and not have to work, so I was able to spend my days researching hypothyroidism, visiting doctors, and resting. Ultimately, I solved my thyroid issues on my own and became a subject expert. A few years later I wrote the bestselling book, *The Paleo Thyroid Solution.*

It turns out that one physical disability outcome helped me solve another physical disability. But by the time I solved my hypothyroidism, I had spent all of my extra money on medical bills; I was in debt and really broke, barely surviving on my disability income. I needed to earn extra money and the only thing I could imagine as a possibility would be to babysit kids or get a part-time job being someone's assistant. I couldn't work 30 or 40 hours a week, but I could work some hours with my hands and I could run errands. Perhaps a busy mother would need me to pick up dry cleaning and pick her kids up from school; I could do that.

The unfortunate financial state that hypothyroidism left me in led me to getting a job working as an assistant to one of the most amazing men I have ever known, Mark Sisson. It was a perfect situation almost designed for my hand disability. I never worked more than 20 hours in a month. In this scenario, just like my previous one in the tech industry, I was maybe the tenth person hired in Mark's fast-growing company. I was on-call to run errands for Mark and his family, booking travel, and taking care of light administrative work. It was perfect for my hand condition and provided me with some extra money on top of my disability payments. I finally had a job for the first in more than 16 years. I felt valued again. I felt some hope.

Through a series of awesome events, Mark eventually published my book on hypothyroidism and as he became substantially busier with the creation of his fast-growing company Primal Kitchen Foods, he eventually entrusted me with hosting his popular podcast, *The Primal Blueprint Podcast*. And suddenly out of nowhere, I had a platform to use my voice. Turns out that my second health disability actually assisted me in finding my way out of dependency on the insurance company. I felt even more hope about my future potential.

However, having a "real job" gave me the perfect excuse to continue hiding my disability, because now I didn't feel as though I had to lie when people asked me how I earned income. I could say I was Mark's assistant, and no one would question how much that paid me. I felt even more comfortable with my big secret because I was able to tell people I had a job. I still had great shame about my disability and I didn't even tell Mark until a few years later. I finally decided to tell him because my shame was preventing me from fully expressing gratitude about how much working for him had changed my life. He had no idea the depths of what it meant to me and my future. I cried my eyes out when I told him, and not surprisingly, I received the kindest, most loving words of encouragement and support.

In 2014, a serious romantic relationship ended with a man who I had no doubt I would marry and be with forever. The only thing (a big thing) I felt was lacking in our relationship was that he could not express himself verbally to me. He *showed me* that he loved me, but there was a lack of true emotional intimacy between us because words of love and appreciation were not expressed. I need words. I would rather have words of love and appreciation than a diamond bracelet. He was emotionally unavailable and I was waiting for him to speak up and express love to me before I did. In my mind, I was waiting for him to express it first so that I would feel safer in sharing my disability story. I was devastated over this break-up, and called my life coach crying. I said, "This seems like such a cruel joke; after all this time and all of this work on myself and on trusting men after my childhood experiences with my dad, I finally meet the man of my dreams and he is perfect, except that he is an emotional robot? WHY WOULD THE UNIVERSE DO THIS TO ME?"

My life coach said something to me that kicked my ass more than anything I had heard in a long time. He asked, "Elle, the universe doesn't play cruel jokes. Did you ever tell him about your disability?" I responded, "No, I never told him." And my coach responded, "Well, then it looks like you are the emotional robot. You were not vulnerable. You were not emotionally available. You were not expressing love. If you expect emotional and verbal intimacy from someone, then you are going to have to give it as well. You need to become more vulnerable in order to connect in this way with a future boyfriend. The thing you are blaming him for as a shortcoming, is actually *your shortcoming*—and you will continue to attract this pattern until you conquer it."

That was a harsh truth to accept, but he was so dead-right I could not defend it. Talk about an amazing coach! In that moment, I knew something had to change with the way I saw myself and my disability story or I would never be able to have an honest, emotionally connected relationship and marriage. Hiding my secret was hurting me, not helping me. So one day I said, "Fuck it, I am just going to start telling people and stop evading questions about my income." My desire for an intimate, connected love relationship propelled me to pull the Band-Aid off and move forward in life. Enough was enough—this was the only area in life where I was suffering and where I didn't have high self-esteem and confidence.

One of my first experiences in testing my newfound bravery was when a fellow podcaster and health coach, Karen Martel, asked me a very direct question: "You do all of these different things, Elle, but what is the main source of your income?" I was immediately mortified. My heart dropped into my stomach and I thought, "I could continue lying to people or dance around this topic and thus repeat this pattern of shame, or I could start practicing right now." So I told Karen the short version of my story. And she said, "Oh my God, Elle. That is exactly why I am a podcaster and a nutritionist, because I injured my hands from being a rolfer (body worker) for fifteen years. I developed severe arthritis in my hands and tendonitis in both my wrists."

What are the odds of that? The very first person (and somewhat of a stranger at the time) who I decide to be brave with also had a hand disability? And in that very instant, I felt less alone. In that very instant, I knew this was the correct path: having no shame about my disability. I got off the phone with Karen and bawled my eyes out in relief and gratitude. I was filled with faith and I felt like the Universe was holding my hand. Turns out, Karen had always wanted to become a nutritionist but she didn't believe she could make a living at it. Her hand injury forced her out of one job and into the career that she was always passionate about. The same goes for me. As a child, I dreamed about being a comedic actor and performer of some kind, but I also didn't think it was a realistic financial endeavor, so I pursued a career in law that turned into a career in the corporate world until the universe cut the golden handcuffs off my wrists and forced me out of one job and ultimately into the career of my dreams.

Very shortly after my conversation with Karen, I interviewed a woman on the Primal Blueprint Podcast name Jezlan Moyet (episode #265). Jezlan is a beautiful international model and one of the hosts of the morning talk show *Good Morning LaLa Land*. Her co-host, Erin Fall Haskell, suggested I interview her because "Jezlan has an interesting health story to share." I had no idea what it was and I didn't ask, I assumed I would find out during the interview. Jezlan and her co-hosts were unaware of my disability at this time.

I was emotionally unprepared for Jezlan's story, and it hit me like a ton of bricks. Jezlan endured a slip-and-fall freak accident that severed nearly every tendon, ligament, and nerve that made her left hand and arm work. After an emergency eight-hour surgery, she awoke thinking she might not be able to use her left hand and arm ever again. In that moment, she could not feel her left hand and thought, "Oh my god, I can't feel my hand. Am I ever going to feel a man put a ring on my finger?"

I put the microphone on mute and starting crying. I could not believe what I was hearing: a mirrored experience of my own fear and shame. Life changed in an instant, from normal to suddenly disabled. The fear, the hopelessness, and the shame. Her thoughts so similar to mine back in San Francisco, wondering, "What man is ever going to want me?" Jezlan and Karen, like me, both have a hand disabilities that you cannot see with your eyes. The three of us look completely "fine" and "normal" on the outside.

My conversations with Karen and Jezlan transpired within the first couple of weeks of my practicing vulnerability and transparency and "coming out" about the shame of my disability. The universe brought me two wonderful women who suffer from a hand disability that altered their lives forever, just as it altered mine. If that isn't a sign to keep on moving forward in the vulnerability/ no shame direction, I don't know what is! Just like my conversation with Karen, in that moment with Jezlan, I felt less alone. And now I know two awesome women to whom I can reach out if need be, who completely understand the stress, the fear, the embarrassment, and the shame associated with being different than the rest of the world, being a person with a physical disability. I think about them often, and I am so grateful that Karen and Jezlan were brought into my life.

I then reached out to a couple of girlfriends who I really liked but had never told my story. I felt badly because they had been vulnerable and open with me about their lives, but I had not been fully connecting with them. I called them each separately and shared my story. I feel even closer to them now. I have no shame about my shame, but I shake my head sometimes thinking about all of those years I allowed it to mess with my life.

This point is worth extra emphasis: If you think you are getting away with hiding and ignoring shame, you are not. It will escape and negatively mess with some part of your life. I am and always have been one of the most confident people I have ever known, yet I had this secret shame in the background, seeping into other areas of my life and wreaking havoc on my self-esteem and confidence in romantic relationships.

Lots of people in this world suffer from disabilities and ailments, and regardless of the severity or type of condition, I guarantee you they have all experienced shame about their situation. Bottom line, it can be embarrassing to have a health issue. It sucks. It shouldn't be that way, but it is. A million people can tell you that you shouldn't be embarrassed or ashamed, but you just are. You are suddenly different than the rest of the human race and now you have to navigate a scary unknown future, which often includes fear about financially providing for yourself.

If you know someone who has endured any health crisis, permanent injury or disability, they might not be talking about their shame. They might be like me and just stuff it all down inside because every time they express sadness and fear over it, people keep telling them, "It's ridiculous, you have nothing to be ashamed about, I don't get it." While that statement is well-meaning, it only makes a disabled person feel more alone, because those words don't *acknowledge* the shame, those words *discount* the person's emotions and experience as ridiculous.

I would encourage you to open up a conversation with these people in your life and help draw them out of this spiral of shame and low self-esteem. Open up a conversation and help that person seek healing. If you are ashamed of anything, you don't have to write a book or produce a YouTube video about whatever it is, but you must deal with it in some way; otherwise it will poke at your confidence and seep into other areas of your life that you assumed were separate and safe. Nothing is separate in our lives. You must step up and move forward in dealing with shame, even if you express it to a support group or a therapist who keeps it confidential.

My disability story is much more intricate than the snapshot I am sharing here. I could write an entire book on the confidence and self-esteem that it takes to successfully battle an insurance company for 20 years. I have learned so many amazing lessons from this journey, and one of them is the incredible empathy I feel towards people who have physical disabilities and medical issues. I am grateful for that. As it turns out, my niece, who was born ten years after I became disabled, was permanently disabled for life when she was just six months old. A freak situation that happens to maybe one-in-a-million children, she was diagnosed with transverse myelitis, a condition that affects the nerves to the lower half of her body. My niece, now 12, uses a wheelchair, a walker, and has to be catheterized in order to urinate. I like to think that perhaps I was meant to experience the intense shame of a disability in order to pay it forward and help my niece navigate what will inevitably be challenges to self-esteem and confidence as she flows into her teenage years and adulthood with a visible, physically-limiting disability. If your children are healthy and have full capacity of their limbs, please take a moment to be grateful.

The level of gratitude that I feel for just possessing arms and hands and no longer being in chronic pain outweighs the flare-ups that I experience. I am not happy and successful *despite* my disability, I am happy and successful *because* of my disability. Sometimes the best gifts in life come wrapped in shit. I would probably not have the awesome life and sense of fulfillment I have now had I not been injured. If I was never injured, I might have two houses and a couple of Porsches in the driveway, but I have a suspicion that I would be rich yet unfulfilled, regretting that I never pursued my passions and dreams because I thought they were financially unrealistic. My plans failed, and I am happy they did because better plans were dropped into my lap.

So, in summary: my hand disability launched me on a 20-year journey to find a way to use my voice. Along the way, I was hit with a second health issue that left me financially strapped, requiring me to seek a job, which led me to Mark Sisson. Working for Mark led me to a platform for using my voice and my writing, which connected right back to my original intention after becoming disabled—pursuing work that utilizes my voice. See how that happened?

All the while I had high confidence and high self-esteem *overall*, but there were major kinks hidden in my armor that had to be buffed out in order to live my best life. And buff them out I did. It wasn't fun at times; I certainly cried a lot about my predicament. I wish the same healing and personal advancement for you, no matter what your challenges are in your life. This too shall pass.

I have enormous gratitude for Michelle Norris, the CEO of Paleo f(x)™ and her husband and co-founder Keith Norris. Paleo f(x)™ is the biggest paleo / primal / ancestral health event in the world which occurs every year in Austin, Texas. They invited me to speak at their event in 2018 about my first book, *The Paleo Thyroid Solution* and in 2019 I asked if I could share a different, very personal story with their audience. While I had previously spoken about my physical disability on a few podcasts prior to Paleo f(x)™, I never went as in-depth as I was able to at their event and I am so grateful for that opportunity. Aside from helping others, it helped heal my shame even further to speak it aloud to a convention full of strangers.

After my speech called *The Shame of Disability and The Disability of Shame* at Paleo f(x)™ 2019, a 26-year-old woman approached me with tears in her eyes. She was diagnosed with rheumatoid arthritis at the age of 19 (often a disease you cannot visibly see) and said that it was very tough for her because her friends didn't have health issues, and they didn't understand what she was going through. She said to me, "I didn't even know who you were, but I just saw people gathering around a stage and I decided to sit down and watch the next speaker. I didn't know what the subject was going to be about. I am so glad I heard your speech, because while I thought I had already dealt with the shame surrounding my medical condition, after hearing your story, I realized that I have much more work to do."

You never know when amazing gifts are going to emerge from the fearful unknown. I am so grateful I that was physically disabled and I am so grateful I was hit with severe hypothyroidism…who says that? But nothing could be more true for me. I understand why people say things like, "Breast cancer was the best thing that ever happened to me." I get it now. It has been my personal experience, and my experience in coaching others, that every time you take a step towards fueling your self-esteem and gaining more confidence, the universe rewards you. If you step away from victimhood and move towards action and perseverance, you will ultimately prevail.

Dealing with shame is critical to your overall self-esteem and becoming *Confident As Fu*k*. Get after it!

PART 5

CREATING YOUR CONFIDENCE REALITY

*You are in physical existence to learn and understand that your
energy, translated into feelings, thoughts and emotions, causes
all experience. There are no exceptions. Once you understand
this you have only to learn to examine the nature of your beliefs,
for these will automatically cause you to feel and think in certain
fashions. Your emotions follow your beliefs. It is not the other
way around.*

- **Seth,** *The Nature of Personal Reality*

I n the fields of intention and positive thinking, quantum physics
is often referenced as a road map for how we can participate
more in the creation of our own reality. Quantum mechanics is
a branch of physics that dictates how the smallest particles in our
universe behave. At this subatomic level, whacky stuff happens;
for example, one electron can be in two places at the same time.
This conundrum alone is enough to realize that there are unknown
possibilities out there we have never considered or thought possible.

One of the principles of quantum mechanics, summed up, is
that nothing is real until it is measured. The spooky thing is, there
are things that we cannot measure but that we know exist because
they have an *observable effect*. Dark matter is an example of this.
Most of our universe is made up of a thing we cannot see and we
cannot measure, but we know it exists because we can observe

its relationship with gravity and other measurable aspects of the universe in space. Dark matter is the main glue that holds our universe together in space, so to speak. So, the main stuff keeping it all together out there is actually invisible and unmeasurable.

There is a magical world of quantum potentials and hidden variables not yet fully grasped by our human minds and scientific instruments. This should be inspiring and encouraging. Once you tap into this unknown and unmeasurable landscape, you will be amazed by how quickly you can change your life and help you manifest faith in the unknown, faith in the unseen, faith in yourself. You can have faith in a god or faith in universal quantum principles. Believing in that which is not yet seen or cannot be measured is the opposite of being skeptical, doubtful, and mistrustful. It is the energy by which new potentials are powered into being.

You can think of practicing intention this way: remember an event in your life that was absolutely wonderful—the birth of a child, a wonderful vacation, perhaps an award you won, an experience you had, anything you felt happy and grateful about in that moment. If I asked you to really get into the emotional feelings of what that past experience felt like—if you closed your eyes and remembered the experience—you could generate the same wonderful feelings that you had at the time of the event. Don't believe me? Everyone reading this has likely dwelled on a past negative and conjured up those feelings. When you want to create something positive in your life, conjure it up. What do you want to manifest? A new job, a new relationship, more income? Instead of just *thinking* about what you want your income to look like, *feel what it would feel like once you get that extra income*. You must focus and generate those emotions within yourself. At first, it seems ridiculous; you might view it as faking a future experience and since you do not have the thing you want yet, it feels like lying to yourself. Please, in this case, go ahead and "lie" to yourself. Because it's not really lying, it's just getting into a positive emotional state for the sake of your future. Try it.

The magic of it is, once you have a session of focusing on the feelings of whatever you want to manifest, you can't walk away from that session and then start telling everyone how broke you are and how you can never get ahead or that it's impossible to get another job. Your emotions need to be matched and encouraged by both thoughts and words. Spending five or 10 minutes daily with your eyes closed and generating and conjuring up positive emotions related to what you want is the key to getting what you want. *Intention is an emotional, feeling endeavor, not an intellectual one.*

Your self-worth, self-esteem, and self-love is subservient to your inner discourse (your thoughts, your words, and subsequently, the *feelings* that follow your thoughts and words). You either have thoughts that enable and empower you towards your dreams, goals, and happiness, or thoughts that do not—it's pretty simple. Consider taking a moment to examine how you talk to yourself about yourself, inside your head. Are you lifting yourself up with encouragement and praise, or disempowering yourself with negative feedback and fear? How do you talk about yourself to others? Are you pro-you, or do you use self-deprecating humor out of low self-esteem or even a false sense of being humble in order to bait people into offering you the praise that you do not give yourself?

We are drawn to and attracted to people who showcase confidence because we intuitively perceive that these people can approach any opportunity with assurance. *We trust their trust in themselves.* Confident people not only appear to be true to themselves, but they enjoy themselves and their own company. Confident people make others feel worthy, because they themselves feel worthy. Confident people feel free and unbound to be themselves, trust their own judgement, and are proud of their character and integrity. This is critical to every aspect of your life, because when you approve of and love who you are in this world, you can move swiftly and peacefully toward success with courage, enthusiasm, and clarity. As you gain more confidence or refine the confidence you already have, you become stronger.

The belief that you deserve to attain love, happiness, and success is an important component of self-esteem. When you feel deserving, you give yourself permission to receive all of the wonderful things that life has to offer. You might think that you truly love yourself, but how do you really know? Just look at the people and experiences that you have attracted in your life. If something in your life is not flowing or feels negative or stressful, those are emotional indicators that something is off between you and your idea of you. Your emotions will steer you in the direction of what needs to be investigated, resolved, or altered.

Your brain has amazing capacities. The brain has trillions of possible connections, each capable of calculating simultaneously— so start viewing your brain as the monster computer it truly is. Your brain has 60,000 thoughts a day, makes trillions of connections, and has the ability to re-wire old, outdated, and negative patterns. Most of us keep thinking the same thoughts, over and over, every day, which leads to the same stories about ourselves and the world, and the same outcomes. You deserve more than this, and it's within your power to change.

What a vacant statement to tell someone, "You just have to think more positively." Sure, but *how* though? How do I get there from here? Successful thinking and the powers of intention manifest when you start consciously changing your words and thoughts about yourself and this world and tap into positive emotions.

Dr. Masaru Emoto is a Japanese researcher famous for his

experiments with water that challenge any pre-existing skeptical relationships between thought and matter. Emoto published several volumes of a work entitled *Messages from Water*, which contain photographs of frozen water crystals using a powerful microscope and high-speed photography in a very cold room. He discovered that the water crystals changed when specific, concentrated thoughts and emotions were directed at them. When he offered loving words to forming water crystals, he observed that the water developed into complex patterns with brilliant color, like snowflakes. Water crystals that had negative, hateful, and fearful thoughts directed towards them had dull-colored and asymmetrical patterns. Our human bodies are comprised of more than 60 percent water, like our earth. Can thoughts, words, and emotions have a similar effect on us? Seems like it's worth a try! As with every scientific endeavor, Dr. Emoto had his share of critics and skeptics, some with valid arguments. Nonetheless, his experiments are fascinating and personally increase my faith in the connection between our emotional intentions and our reality.

We can have great control over the *experience* and *perception* of our lives and work on creating a reality we desire, but we cannot always control the parameters, details, and specifics. Things happen beyond our choice or control. Sometimes the unknown and the unseen and even the real "Oh shit," moments end up being more in favor of your dreams than what you could have imagined or planned on your own. Some called it co-creation with the universe, some call it "God's work." Who cares what we call it, I can tell you this: it is worth the effort to experiment with using your thoughts and emotions in the spirit of creating your own reality, using the power of intention. Try it. What do you have to lose? Is what you are doing now working for you?

The subconscious mind is made up of genetic drives and

memories. With repetitive thoughts or actions, habits are created, and they can be positive by enabling you to make generalizations to form expectations. You know the cliché, "It's like riding a bike." At first, it's daunting, then it becomes familiar, then automatic. If you start to believe that a memory or habit is an inherent fundamental program within you, that will manifest as your reality. For example, by continually finding yourself in work environments that feel difficult, you might draw the conclusion that "all companies suck, all work is tough," and that becomes its own self-fulfilling prophecy and part of your belief system, and therefore your reality. I know lots of people who do not feel their work environments are challenging at all—so do they have a magic wand? Nope, they just look at their lives differently. It is time to believe in the potential of unknown awesome possibilities.

CONFIDENCE IN PHYSICAL AND MENTAL HEALTH

You yourself, as much as anyone in the entire universe deserve your love and affection.

- **Buddha**

If thoughts from your mind and the emotions that follow are key to developing self-esteem and confidence and creating the life you want, becoming mentally and physically healthy is essential. You need to get your body and brain functioning at optimal capacity. Everything we put in our mouths has an effect on our brain and body. As a certified Primal Health Coach, I firmly believe in an ancestral paradigm for health, longevity, and wellness, but you can also be a vegan or vegetarian and be *Confident As Fu*k*. I am not saying that adopting a paleo paradigm is necessary, but if you suffer from low energy or don't feel like you have the mental focus or physical vitality that you want, it could have an effect on your emotions in a way that can stifle your confidence and cause depression. If you don't feel good in your brain and body, please check out what our ancestors did and what our DNA has to say about how we should move, eat, and live. In my first book, *The Paleo Thyroid Solution,* I define and explain this ancestral health model.

For most of my life I struggled with the symptoms of depression and spent decades on anti-depressants. However, I refused to accept this diagnosis and spent most of my life looking for the root cause. Finally, an IgG test revealed a severe sensitivity to dairy and grains, causing a great amount of inflammation, and the complex chemical cascade that ultimately causes symptoms of depression. Once I removed all dairy and grains, my symptoms were nearly gone and I was able to wean off medication. It was a massive game changer, to say the least.

- **Holly Perkins, author of** *Lift To Get Lean,* **and voted "Top Trainer to follow" by** *Shape Magazine*

Excerpt from The Paleo Thyroid Solution by Elle Russ

As humans, we are all born with a DNA map to health and happiness. In fact, every species was born with their own DNA maps. Unfortunately, over the past 10,000 years, humans have thrown away that map and unknowingly taken a detour in the wrong direction, which opened the door and invited in the diseases of modern life.

Ever since paleo became a popular buzz word, people have been grossly misinterpreting it on a variety of levels. Paleo, primal, ancestral, and evolutionary health are all terms that describe the same movement. The biggest misconception about a paleo lifestyle is that it is merely a list of foods you can or cannot eat. This could not be further from the truth. The paleo/primal lifestyle is different from any other eating strategy out there today. It enables you to get off the carbohydrate-dependency hamster wheel, which is the cause of so many diseases, and allows you to transition into a fat-burning machine. Our society is crippled with a Type 2 Diabetes epidemic and an array of other metabolic dysfunctions, autoimmune disorders, and mental disorders. People suffering from these conditions have found success in fully reversing these types of conditions through following a high fat, moderate protein, low carb approach. I am one of those people. A big step further into the ancestral world, and we are witnessing the rise of followers of the carnivore diet (A strict nose-to-tail diet devoid of vegetables, fruits, and all carbohydrates) has helped people solve digestive issues, autoimmune conditions, and more.

WHAT IS A SUGAR-BURNER?

If you are a sugar-burner, your body is dependent on (i.e., addicted to) fueling itself on glucose. If you are a sugar-burner, you trained your body to function this way; many people do this unwittingly based on flawed, conventional diet wisdom that instructs people to eat every two to three hours and/or adopt a low-fat/high-carbohydrate diet. The reason so many people cannot lose weight or maintain weight loss without struggling is that they are sugar-burners.

You are a sugar-burner if:

* You cannot go more than eight waking hours without eating because you will

* get cranky, have a drop in physical or mental energy, or experience other negative symptoms

* You have hypoglycemia
* You struggle to lose weight
* You struggle to keep weight off
* You cannot get food off of your mind, and you have food obsessions/addictions
* You crave sugary foods, and it takes a ton of willpower to refuse the cravings
* You crave grain-based carbohydrates like bread, rice, cereal, and baked goods
* You can't seem to burn fat
* You are hungry every two to five hours
* You have drops in energy during the day

I used to be royally obsessed with food. At one point, I thought about joining Overeaters Anonymous because I didn't understand why I was so food-obsessed. I couldn't go more than three to four hours without eating, or I would get very cranky and feel exhausted and mentally drained. Like many people, I thought the "eat every two-to-three hours" philosophy was the healthiest eating strategy, based on the information I read in almost every diet book on the market. And it certainly seemed in line with the symptoms I had when I did not follow that routine, so I believed the strategy had merit. However, at the time I didn't realize that there was a much easier and healthier way: eating the way our bodies were genetically programmed to operate.

WHAT IS A FAT-BURNER?

If you are a fat-burner, you can use the fat from your diet and the fat stored in your body to fuel yourself. Fat has been the primary fuel source for humans for 2.5 million years, both from storage and as the predominant macronutrient in the human diet. In fact, it was energy-rich, high-fat animal products (particularly omega-3 fatty acids) that facilitated the development of a more complex brain and allowed humans to branch out from their predominantly vegetarian ape cousins to eventually rise to the top of the food chain.

Our genetic makeup is still the same as our hunter-gatherer ancestors who lived 50,000 years ago. Our bodies were designed to burn fat, not glucose, as a preferred fuel.

Our preference for fat-burning conflicts with the government food pyramid, which suggests that carbohydrates should form the foundation of a healthy diet. The government food pyramid recommends eating six to eleven servings of grains per day and two to four servings of fruit, along with limiting fat intake and other irrational suggestions that lead to health issues. Our modern high-carbohydrate, grain-based diet has sparked a dependency on external carbohydrates for energy at the expense of efficient fat metabolism.

We are the only living things on the face of the Earth who have "food issues." Animals in the wild don't require food every two to three hours to maintain energy and stamina. Humans have burned fat as their primary source of energy throughout human evolution. Our hunter-gatherer ancestors were not only lean and fit, but they did not have diseases of modern life, such as type 2 diabetes, hypothyroidism, and autoimmune disorders, until the abrupt transition to a grain-based diet. The agricultural move-ment—and the decline of human health—entered the picture ten thousand years ago, once humans settled down in one area, stopped wandering, and started to domesticate animals. Dairy came on the scene about seven thousand years ago, and sugar showed up only two hundred years ago.

A high-carbohydrate, high-insulin-producing diet inhibits fat metabolism, making you dependent upon regular carbohydrate feedings in order to sustain mental and physical energy. This promotes a lifelong accumulation of excess body fat, an exhaustion of your adrenal glands' fight-or-flight stress responses, along with emotional tribulations related to eating. Living life as a sugar-burner is a never-ending struggle to balance calories in with calories out. A grain-infused, high-carbohydrate diet also promotes inflammation and free radical damage in the body, accelerating the aging process and contributing to all health problems, including heart disease and cancer.

Our hunter-gatherer ancestors ate a diet high in animal flesh and animal fat and low in carbohydrates and sugar. Did you know that humans can live their entire lives without ever eating a single carbohydrate, but we could not survive without protein and fat? Not only will our bodies produce glucose on their own, but excess protein goes through a process called gluconeogenesis, which converts excess protein into glucose. So in times of overeating animal flesh in the wild, human bodies would turn that excess protein into carbohydrates.

We were all born with a perfect genetic formula to live long, happy lives and spend our time in lean, fit bodies with an abundance of mental and physical energy. The introduction of grains, sugar, dairy, and excess carbohydrate consumption has, over time, turned millions of people into sugar-burners who are glucose dependent. A sugar-burning existence will put you at risk for developing food addictions, hypoglycemia, insulin resistance, type 2 diabetes, adrenal gland issues, thyroid issues, and more.

You are a fat-burner if:

* You can go more than eight to ten or even twenty-four

hours without eating food and still maintain physical/mental energy and stamina with zero desire for food

* You effortlessly lose weight and maintain weight loss without mental or physical struggles

* You "forget" about food and are not obsessed with your next meal

* You don't crave sugar or grain-based foods

Like our hunter-gatherer ancestors, a person who is fat adapted can go eight to twenty-four hours without eating and still have full mental focus and physical energy. When is the last time you went more than five hours without food and didn't have a meltdown? It is rare for millions of Americans. Furthermore, the consumption of grains can lead to nutrient deficiencies and can cause/ignite autoimmune disorders such as Hashimoto's, arthritis, and more.

However, when people adopt a paleo lifestyle correctly, they experience a freedom that only fat-burners understand. Being fat adapted is an amazing and wonderful life that I wish I had known about over a decade ago.

In order to reap the benefits of a paleo/primal lifestyle, it is necessary to transition your body from a glucose-dependent sugar-burner to a fat-adapted fat-burner. The biggest challenge in this transition is that it takes about three to four weeks of mental willpower to succeed. You don't have to lift a finger in terms of exercise in order to make this transition, but it does require dedication as your body becomes un-addicted to glucose as its main source of fuel. During this period of transition, your brain will trick you into thinking you are hungry, and mental/physical energy lapses can occur. Your brain is an addict that is going through glucose/carbohydrate withdrawal and is trying to trick you into consuming its drug of choice—sugar.

Becoming fat adapted is the process of breaking an addiction cycle. One month of mental willpower for a lifetime of freedom was worth it to me. Becoming fat adapted not only changed my body, brain, and spirit, it enabled me to reduce my thyroid medication. Adopting a paleo lifestyle inherently addresses all of the underlying causes of adrenal fatigue and blood sugar issues which helps your endocrine system function more efficiently, including thyroid hormone metabolism.

Keys to Paleo Fat Adaptation

* Consume quality paleo/primal foods and manage carbohydrates (under 150 grams of total carbohydrates per day unless you are a professional athlete. For women or smaller people like me, under 100 grams of total carbohydrates per day or lower).

* Low-intensity exercise combined with an occasional sprint session

* Lifestyle: prioritizing adequate sleep, sunlight, fresh air, and stress reduction/managementGeneral paleo/primal ratio: high fat/moderate protein/low carbohydrate

* All four components of paleo/primal living must be adopted in order to achieve success in all areas, including weight loss, adrenal health, and blood glucose management.

"As a functional medicine practitioner using food-as-medicine, abundance is just as powerful as restriction, as is focusing as much on removing pro-inflammatory, mood-disturbing ingredients as you do on consuming abundant therapeutic foods to tonify and support the body. Start with priorities on gluten, corn, soy, sugar, and dairy while adjusting the carbohydrate

level in your diet to support low regulated blood sugar levels and production of ketones. When the brain is running on high-octane fuel of ketones supported by essential nutritional compounds without inflammatory distraction, brain chemistry and mood stability have a reciprocal relationship for favorable, whole-body physiology including positive outcomes in your regulatory para-sympathetic function impacting thyroid, adrenals, and hormones while promoting a mellow, grounded mental state."

- Ali Miller, RD, LD, CDE integrative dietitian and author of *The Anti-Anxiety Diet* **and host of The Naturally Nourished podcast**

BE CAREFUL ON THE SEND

We have all sent a text message, an email, or made a phone call and later regretted it. Sometimes our reactionary mind gets the best of us and we take a step forward in aggressive communication that we later regret. Next time you are ready to fire off a contentious email, text or phone call...stop. Let 24 hours go by. Sleep on it. Email it to yourself and then re-visit sending it the next morning. More often than not, when we take a breather and allow ourselves to work through the reactionary emotions of these situations we discover more productive ways of communicating (hello editing!). Taking time to sit back, reflect, go within, move through the stages of ego and negative emotions—that is the highest road. Simmer on it and be *careful on the send.*

STOP REASONING YOUR DEFEAT

Back in the day, my friend Jenny was awaiting college acceptance letters. When she was deferred for early-acceptance at her first choice of colleges (meaning that she had to wait a few more months for a decision), she immediately started to reason her future denial letter. Jenny started to give reasons why that school might not be best for her after all, like maybe it was too far from home. She was reasoning her potential future defeat rather than projecting her future acceptance. Why do we do this? To make the blow of a potential future rejection sync with our fragile egos? Why would we immediately cling to a potential loss, versus focusing on a potential win? We need to change this. What happened to keeping hope alive and fighting for what you want, regardless of receiving an initial denial?

I disliked the first university I attended. I didn't have much of a choice in colleges after graduation from high school because I had been expelled; no doubt my college applications were at the bottom of every pile of admission offices all over the country. I decided to transfer schools my sophomore year, and I got so much heat from my mother. "But you already have a scholarship!" and, "The teachers like you," and "It's just another two years, stick it out," and "What if you don't get accepted anywhere!?" and "Why don't you just do a year abroad, and then when you return, you'll only have one year left at that place!" and my response to her was, "Fuck. No. I don't care if I have to take a year off before going to another school. I am not returning, under any circumstance to this school. Doesn't matter what you suggest, I am not coming back here." When I applied to transfer universities my sophomore year, I was initially denied admission to my first choice of schools, The University of California at Santa Cruz.

How did I accept that rejection? I appealed the decision and continually persevered in convincing UC Santa Cruz to accept me. Nothing was going to stop me from getting into that school. Are you surprised that it worked? As a result of my not accepting defeat, I am incredibly proud to be an alumna of UC Santa Cruz, referred to as a *Banana Slug*, our school mascot. Let us embrace the old adage, "If you first don't succeed, try, try again." Transferring to UC Santa Cruz and moving to California was one of the best decisions of my entire life. Occasionally I look back and imagine a parallel existence where I never spoke up and stood my ground with my mother, and I get goosebumps of gratitude for my confidence and self-esteem. Still, to this day, I am so grateful that I was *Confident As Fu*k* about my choices and plans. Occasionally, when my mother vehemently challenges a decision of mine, I remind her of the above scenario how grateful I am for following my gut and my goals back then. She's awesome, and she gets it.

If you really want it, get after it. And if you don't get accepted into a school or a program, do yourself a favor and appeal that rejection whether they have an appeal process or not. There is nothing to lose in being persistent, and everything to gain.

HUMILITY? GET OVER IT

Some people believe there is a great merit and holy virtue in what they think of as humility. Therefore to be proud of oneself seems a sin and in that frame of reference true affirmation of the self is impossible. Genuine self-pride is the loving recognition of your own integrity and value...True humility is based upon this affectionate regard for yourself, plus the recognition that you live in a universe in which all other beings also possess this undeniable individuality and self-worth. False humility tells you that you are nothing. It often hides a distorted, puffed-up, denied self-pride, because no man or woman can really accept a theory that denies personal self-worth. Fake humility can cause you to tear down the value of others, because if you accept no worth in yourself you cannot see it in anyone else either. True self-pride allows you to perceive the integrity of your fellow human beings and permits you to help them use their strengths.

- Seth, from *The Nature of Personal Reality*

If you feel uncomfortable when a *Confident As Fu*k* person declares their pride in themselves and touts their abilities—because you see it as boastful or a lack of humility—it's likely that *you* have issues with your own self-esteem and confidence. When I hear someone genuinely tooting their own horn, I smile, instantly proud of them and think, "Fuck yeah, right on girl— own it!" It makes me so happy to see and hear people exuding confidence. Some people were raised to not speak about their accomplishments, and if that is you, that's just more parental garbage that needs to be taken to the dump.

CONFIDENCE PITFALL: RESCUING OTHERS

Alphas are hard on the outside, messy on the inside. Alphas are very inaccessible and intimidating to most people. But people love us in a crisis because we are crisis mangers, we are planners, we are amazing analyzers and super independent. So, if something is messed up, people want to throw an alpha at it, because we are fixers. Alphas also have a life cycle. First, we fight—we are willing to fight with people to make things work. We are going to force it to come out right and be the way we want. We constantly engineer outcomes. The second phase of the cycle is control; we try convincing people by buying their affection instead of fighting. So we fix everything for everybody (because we are rescuers) and over-give. Unsurprisingly, we cannot get our own stuff done and then don't feel supported. So we don't write our book or get our business plan finished because our niece is in trouble, our husband needs something, and so on...and that becomes the noble excuse. So, how do we break free of this cycle? By doing the things alphas don't want to do, the foundation work: the self-love, the self-trust, and the self-worth. When you don't give it to yourself first, you can never get it from other people. Trying to earn it...it just doesn't work.

- Tanya Stewart, Esq., Alpha Life Coach

Outwardly confident people are often referred to as alpha. I am a proud alpha woman. Some people misunderstand alphas as boastful, braggadocios, over-the-top personalities, but those are misconceptions. Alphas are confident in their abilities, yet they often have classic pitfalls that need to be addressed to gain more confidence and self-esteem.

Help the worthy, not the needy. Are you too busy encouraging and rescuing others and helping them navigate their goals over your own? I had this pitfall for many years: a pattern of rescuing unworthy people and attempting to help them build self-esteem, until I realized that I had limited time and bandwidth to work on my own projects, goals, and dreams. How much time are you spending in conversations with friends or colleagues that won't take action to propel themselves forward? You must give up the desire to rescue people, so that you can move onward and upward and not remain in a stagnant place of only cheerleading others. Stop answering the phone, stop engaging in conversations that feel yucky or go nowhere. End the need to be the hero in someone else's journey.

Because I have writing skills, friends have asked me to review things they write. College essays, letters to insurance companies, cover letters, and so on. With one of my friends, Dan, I started to notice that I was enabling his insecurities about writing because every time he presented me with something, I would completely re-write it for him. Dan never had to step up to the plate because I always swooped in and did the work for him. One time, he called me because he was writing a letter to an insurance company and felt insecure about it. Instead of writing it for him per my usual pattern, I said, "Dan, you're smart. Go and write a substantial draft of a letter that you think is presentable to the insurance company and I will look it over when you're done." Dan sent me the letter, and it was perfect! In fact, he didn't even need my help at all! How much time had I wasted over the years with this stuff when all along, he had the ability to do it himself? Not only did Dan gain confidence in his abilities that day, but I was forever released from rescuing him in these situations. By rescuing him in the past, I was enabling and even fueling his lack of confidence in an ability that it turns out he was actually good at, and now suddenly confident in.

Don't enable people just because you can get it done faster, or because you think you can do it better than they can. People will surprise you if you allow them. If you want to truly help increase people's confidence, make them try it first, and then be available to help only if they need it. And sometimes, don't make yourself available at all.

Confident alphas like myself often attract people who need more confidence and self-esteem, but it is not a one-way friendship. There is a complementary relationship here. Less confident people are often really good at receiving. They are good at receiving love, at asking for and receiving help from others, and they also trust others to be in control. Alphas often have weaknesses in those areas, because we prefer to be in control and find it tough to ask for and accept help, which can get us into trouble. Alphas also have issues with vulnerability—I definitely did. Because I was so strong and confident, I saw displaying emotions and expressing fears or vulnerabilities as weak. No alpha wants to appear weak, so it's harder for us to open up to people and that is why we are often inaccessible. Confidence and vulnerability seem like they oppose each other, yet I would argue that *the most confident people are good at being vulnerable* because they truly have no shame or worry about what other people think. That is confidence and self-esteem to the max. Expressing vulnerability and being more open to receiving help from others is where alphas can learn from their friends. Alphas help others speak up and cultivate self-esteem and confidence in their independence, stand their ground, declare their worth, perhaps get out of codependent situations. And on the other hand, we alphas need to sit back and learn the benefits of vulnerability, active listening, diplomacy, and receiving love and assistance. Alphas have a lot to learn from the people we incorrectly assume are weaker; they have invaluable lessons to teach us.

SPEAKING UP, A LITTLE AT A TIME

There is no way my life would be as awesome as it is if I did not possess the ability to speak up in life. Speaking up is a critical form of honesty, and honesty builds trust. You can't live a happy life if you won't speak up for what you need and want. You must speak up in order to:

* Draw healthy boundaries with people
* Go after and get what you want in life
* Be vulnerable
* Connect with others
* Share a story that could help others

* Declare your worth

* Truly love yourself

* Be an incredible friend, son, daughter, parent, employee, cousin, spouse, and so on

Silence can be received as approval. You may think being quiet will keep you from conflict, but it often yields the opposite result and causes great turmoil. It can lead to people-pleasing, hidden resentments, and covert contracts that inevitably backfire.

John is a perfect example of how speaking up, even about small things in life, can be a major component of building inner confidence. John is a man with very high confidence in many things. He is tall, handsome, and fit as a fiddle, and he knows it. He spear-fishes in the middle of open oceans all around world which a very intense, dangerous and rigorous sport. He trained himself to hold his breath underwater for five minutes; he's ultra-confident spearing a fish and then wrangling the 150-pound sea creature out of the ocean. John is also an anesthesiologist and has high confidence in his job: he puts people to sleep for surgeries and has to bring them back alive! You might think John is the most alpha, badass *Confident As Fu*k* man on earth. But he is not—in fact he is quite the opposite, on the inside, about many things.

John had just finished washing the outside of his entire house by hand. He soon learned that his neighbor (a very kind, friendly man), was about to have some workers pressure-wash his house. John was immediately worried and already annoyed that his neighbor might get his house dirty again. For a week, John lamented in his head and to me, because he couldn't bring himself to have a conversation with his neighbor about it. John can jump confidently into the ocean with sharks and administer a spinal tap without hesitation, but he can't bring himself to speak a few sentences to a neighbor. Yikes.

And because he was too insecure to speak up, he did what a lot of people with low self-esteem do in these scenarios: he started building up resentment and frustration for something that had not even transpired yet. He began having virtual arguments in his head with the neighbor, projecting that this very sweet man would suddenly become an asshole, and cultivating annoyance and dislike for his neighbor for doing something he didn't even do yet.

Here's my conversation with John:

ELLE: "John, your neighbor is very nice and has never given you any reason to think he's an asshole, right?"

JOHN: "No, he is the nicest guy, definitely not an asshole."

ELLE: "Ok, so what worries you about having a conversation with him?"

JOHN: "I don't know, I don't want him to think I'm a dick."

ELLE: "So your hesitation is really about *what you think he might think of you* for asking him to be careful when washing his house, and not because you think he is going to be mean to you?"

JOHN: "I guess so. I just feel bad, he's so nice. I don't want to cause any problems."

ELLE: "Do you know for a fact that your simple request would cause problems between the two of you?"

JOHN: "No, but I feel bad."

ELLE: "Why do you feel bad?"

JOHN: "Because he's really nice and I just don't want him to think I'm an asshole."

ELLE: "You are worried and feel bad because *you are too nice*. Being too nice is people-pleasing, and people-pleasing is lying. You are holding back on getting what you want because you are worried about what someone will think of you. But if you don't say anything, and your house gets dirty, you are going to be annoyed and pissed *at him*—not only changing your vibration, but changing how you feel about your neighbor, and you will be the one who actually caused an issue that wasn't there. And just like a victim, you will think, 'See, I knew it! He dirtied up my house and now I have to re-wash it!'"

JOHN: "Oh shit. Yeah, that sucks."

ELLE: "You have two choices. You either say something ahead of time to prevent your house from getting dirty, or you say nothing and risk the chance that your house might get dirty and you will have to wash it again, and also be annoyed about it. The first choice will likely solve the issue immediately. If you speak up and he tells you to fuck off, then okay—you learned that your neighbor is not nice after all. If you speak up and it goes well, then great! No bad vibes on the block and you won't have to re-wash your house: problem solved."

JOHN: "What do I say? I don't want to come across mean."

ELLE: "How about a straight-up factual request? Something like, 'Hey neighbor, I know your workers are going to be washing your house later this week. I just finished washing mine, is there any way you could have your workers set up some tarps or be extra careful not to let the dirt and debris get onto my house?"

JOHN: "That seems simple."

ELLE: "It is simple, it is clear, and it has no emotion behind it, no judgements—it's just a factual statement and a reasonable request. Try it."

John went to his neighbor and had the conversation—and his neighbor responded exactly as I assumed he would.

Neighbor: "Absolutely John, and if for some reason my workers get dirt all over your house, I will have them pressure wash yours too."

John called me, and you would think he had just won the lottery!

JOHN: "It was so easy! No problem at all, what a great guy!"

John is confident in many areas of life, but talking to people with regards to getting his needs met is not one of them. John also finds himself in romantic relationships that are unhealthy and codependent. He doesn't speak up for his needs and desires in a relationship and then lets resentment build up, just like with his neighbor. At work, John agrees to extra shifts and never puts his foot down about saying no, and then he gets resentful of the people in charge for his stressful work hours. He gets resentful of people for shit he could have prevented had he just spoken up from the beginning. John's working on it, just like the rest of us.

You can be the most fearless, confident person at many things while other areas of your life suffer because you don't apply the same level of confidence and self-esteem. In order to be happy, the goal is to have your high self-esteem and confidence aligned and in sync in all areas. John *appears* confident because of his hobbies and profession, yet his interpersonal life is sometimes a disaster because he does not speak up for himself. It's a lesson that confidence in one area of life does not equate to true confidence in all areas. Being truly *Confident As Fu*k* is all-encompassing.

Our life is about interacting with others. You must speak up to get what you want, from the boardroom to the bedroom. Truly confident people take leaps of faith; they take action. Leaps of faith include those uncomfortable "It never hurts to ask," and "It never hurts to try," moments. So much bravery and confidence can exist in small steps, like conversations with a neighbor. Being *Confident As Fu*k* is not about being a tactless, harsh asshole with no compassion for others—it's about being aligned with who you really are and accepting your shortcomings, knowing that it does not change your overall self-worth. Short of being in a dangerous situation, when you don't speak up but you want to, you are not cultivating integrity and authenticity within yourself. Truly confident people are authentic, they take action, and they speak up.

MOVING PAST SHAME

Another example of a person who is seemingly confident on the outside, but a self-esteem disaster on the inside, is Ethan. Ethan has his own law firm, a few really nice properties, two cars, lots of fun toys and sports equipment, and a successful social life—he seems like quite the catch! He is a smart, outgoing, animated guy with a good sense of humor. Ethan exudes confidence on the surface, but on the inside he suffers greatly with the shame of severe erectile dysfunction. The shame of his condition, in part, is that often people with erectile dysfunction can't achieve erections with others, but sometimes can through watching porn—so they become addicted to porn, which continually widens the divide between real life relationships and fantasy. To make matters worse, he also has genital herpes. As you can imagine, having severe erectile dysfunction along with a transmittable STD results in a mountain of shame to contend with.

Ethan's shame was so disabling that in order to make himself feel better, he would try to dig into the psyche of his girlfriends to find what they were ashamed of. In the spirit of transparency, he would prompt women to share their deepest feelings or secrets with him. On the surface, it seems like a lovely, open-hearted endeavor to connect with another soul in an intimate way, but that was not Ethan's motivation. He wanted to gather information in an attempt to offset his own shame about his personal issues. Once Ethan found out what his current girlfriend was ashamed of, he would gaslight them by intentionally triggering them about their insecurities. He would make a seemingly innocuous, subtle remark that he knew would spark their insecurities, with the goal of making them feel less-than so that he could feel better about himself and exude a type of emotional control over them.

And every single time, he would get busted.

The girlfriends would eventually grow suspicious of controlling comments and gaslighting and would question his behavior, after which he would immediately bail. This happened over and over and his relationships only lasted about two months, because no one can keep that shit up and not expect it to backfire. I told Ethan that when he finally takes control of his self-esteem and shame, he will be in a position to have a healthy relationship with a woman without fear of rejection or a need to feel superior. No one can acquire true confidence through emotional head games and manipulation amidst a backdrop of shame and fear of rejection.

CONFIDENCE IN PUBLIC SPEAKING AND PERFORMING

Performance confidence merely takes practice, and over time I believe anyone can get comfortable with it if that is your goal. In 1999, I took a risk and mustered up the courage to write and perform sketch comedy for the first time. I was really nervous. Thirty minutes before my very first show, I ran to the bathroom with horrible gas cramps and pooped my brains out. It happened again thirty minutes before the second show, and also the third show, and finally stopped before the fourth and final show. This is what performers call the "pre-show shits" and it happens to many first-time actors and performers. It goes away over time, with practice and confirming self-talk. Audition and performance anxiety is common and confidence on stage in front of an audience is like any skill: the more you do it, the more confirmable it becomes. Just because I am *Confident As Fu*k* doesn't mean that I don't have moments of self-doubt or performance jitters before a speech, but I combat it with self-talk that usually goes something like this: "Hey, you asked for this life. You signed up for this. You are going to go out there and kill it. You have to. You can't turn back now. This is what you wanted, so you better get over yourself and rock this mo-fo." More often than not, I get excited about performing, speaking, and being interviewed—and thankfully, I no longer have the pre-show-shits.

Even if you have no designs to be an actor or performer of any kind, taking an improvisation class is one of the scariest, most awkward, and most rewarding adventures you can undertake, and it really helps with overcoming shyness and fear of public speaking. Improvisation classes are often very safe, welcoming spaces to make an ass out of yourself and not worry what others think of you. Improv is not about being funny as much as it is about thinking on your feet in the moment.

Any seasoned improv teacher will instruct the class that failure is completely welcome and expected because there are no mistakes, really; it's about learning how to play the game as well as you can, not about cracking jokes or getting it right. I performed improv for many years and one thing that is glaringly apparent is that planning doesn't work. Sometimes improv actors will try to plan a scene or a funny zinger ahead of time; this often fails and is obvious to the audience. Improv is a great way to get out of your head and into the present moment; it also helps you communicate and makes you a better story-teller. It's scary at first (and super embarrassing and awkward), but I think it is one of the best and least-expensive ways to build confidence.

CONFIDENCE IN THE WORKPLACE

I used to interview and hire people for a living, and I found that the confident applicants who declared their worth and their value without hesitation usually got the job. Why? Because I could *feel their confidence* in their ability to do the job, and confidence often overrides skill and experience—employers are sometimes even willing to pay more than originally budgeted for such people. As an employer, I would rather hire someone with less experience and skills but more personal confidence, because I know the value of that trait: they are on time, proactive problem-solvers, have good communication skills, are quick-learners, and respond well to stressful situations. To an employer, confident people are valuable because confidence equates to higher *potential*.

You must first become confident in your ideas before you can confidently present them to a group. Often a person is confident about an idea but lacks the confidence to speak up and share it. If you are not confident in the idea itself, work on coming up with something you do feel confident about first. In the workplace, you can present it like, "Hey, I have something I would like to add to this conversation," or "I have an idea, what about…" If you get shut down, at least you spoke up and made the effort and you can try again at the next meeting. If you keep getting shut down, either your ideas aren't great and need to be fleshed out, or you need to look for another job. Speaking up and being confident in the workplace could mean the difference between you getting a raise or promoted, or not.

CONFIDENCE IN DATING

Confidence is an attractive quality for both men and women. I have been on many first dates in my life, and when I sense that a man lacks self-esteem and confidence, it instantly knocks the attraction-factor down. I have heard comments from men like, "I think I'm smart, but probably not smart enough for you. You are like really, really smart," or, "You are so funny! I'm not as funny as you, I'm afraid I won't be able to make you laugh," and so on. How is someone supposed to respond to those low-confidence remarks?

My friend Gina was online dating and vented, "Ugh, online dating is so depressing, I emailed a bunch of men and got zero responses. It makes me feel bad. It's a lot of rejection to deal with." I countered, "Gina, what if you found out that all of the men you contacted were either convicted felons, wife-abusers, had major mental illnesses, or were raging alcoholics? Would you feel rejected or would you be relieved that you never heard back from them?" Gina said, "Well obviously I wouldn't want that." I responded, "Really? Because your feelings of rejection are saying otherwise. Your feelings of rejection are based on what complete strangers might think of you—and it's not even what they truly think of you! You are projecting onto complete strangers *what you think they might think of you.* Why would you put the power of your own self-worth in the hands of anyone, much less a stranger on the internet whom you know nothing about?"

So many people go into first dates hoping that the other person will like them. The *Confident As Fu*k* paradigm shift involves moving into curiosity, and adopting the following attitude: "Let me see if I like this person and feel that they're worth my time." This is all about you and what you think of the other person; anything short of this stance is reflecting low self-esteem. The old paradigm is just you handing your self-worth over to a stranger you know nothing about, and that is insanity. Enough of that.

CONFIDENCE IN THE BEDROOM

If you are in tune with your sexuality, then you have specific desires you want met by your partner. Your sexual needs cannot manifest if you don't speak up. I don't care whether you want to be tied up and whipped or whether you like dirty talk, I have no judgements about what you're into—but you won't get any of them if you don't communicate. It is important to be on the same page with your sexual partner. Couples can run into problems when sexual desires are expressed as criticisms, or voiced at the wrong time or in the wrong way. Sex is supposed to be fun, but sometimes giving instructions to another can cause anxiety or kill the vibe. Self-identified "SexPert" Susan Bratton has this to say about getting what you want in the bedroom:

Sometimes you know just what you want during sex... more frequently all you know is that what you are experiencing isn't quite right or it could be better. Add in the fact that women are hormonally cyclical, which affects how they want to be stimulated in any given moment, then layer on the effect of testosterone making men more steady-state, more goal-oriented during lovemaking and overly confident in their bedroom skills. Add to that the fear women have of hurting a man's ego by speaking up. These norms result in couples who drift apart physically, enjoying less sex over time. How can you disrupt this time-worn groove and get on what I like to call the upward pleasure spiral where sex keeps getting better your whole life long? By using a bedroom communication skill dubbed, "The Sexual Soulmate Pact." This simple agreement between lovers encourages and rewards pillow talk. When you appreciate the changeable nature of our animal bodies (instead of taking feedback as failure);

when you relish requests as the path to becoming even better at lovemaking together; when you're on the same pleasure team (understanding our changeable animal bodies); when you thank your partner each time they express refinements to encourage them to keep a steady stream of communication happening... THAT'S when you ride up the pleasure spiral together.

- Susan Bratton, "Trusted Hot Sex Advisor to Millions"

CONFIDENCE AND KIDS

First and foremost, I would like to make a plea that people, especially men, start to compliment little girls and young women on things other than their physical appearance. Rather than "You look so pretty," or "I love your hair," or "What a cute dress!" Let's say, "What a smart observation!" or "That was a very kind thing you did for your friend," or "You are so smart!" These are the kind of compliments that fuel true confidence. Looks-based comments are predominately directed towards girls and young women while little boys and young men tend to get compliments about their intelligence and accomplishments. It's easy to find ways to compliment girls on their intelligence or character, not their appearance.

Here's a good illustration about confidence and kids. One day, I took a friend's daughter to a pool for a swim. As we approached the pool, which had about five or six other kids her age playing in it, we chatted:

SARAH: "I get nervous around other kids."

ELLE: "Oh really, why is that?"

SARAH: "I don't know, I just get nervous and anxious."

ELLE: "Ok, but why? Why are you nervous? Are you afraid of these kids?"

SARAH: "I'm afraid of being bullied."

ELLE: "Ok, let's talk about that. Have you been bullied at school?"

SARAH: "A few times."

ELLE: "By kids who are your friends, or by other kids at school?"

Sarah proceeded to tell me some bullying stories and one of them really stung me. Sarah said that she normally sits with a group of kids at lunch, but she wanted to go sit with another kid elsewhere so she said to the table, "If it's okay, I am going to go sit with Amy." (Her first mistake was asking permission). The girls who are supposed to be her friends at the table said, "Well, you can sit with Amy on Tuesdays and Thursdays, but that's it." Thankfully, Sarah had a *Confident As Fu*k* friend at the table who said, "Um, no. You are not her boss you are not going to tell Sarah when she can or cannot sit with someone else." I loved that kid!

I proceeded to talk to Sarah about speaking up for herself and not allowing her power of choice to be taken away by someone else. It's not enough to tell a kid who is being bullied, "Oh just ignore them." It affects them; we are social animals and a big part of school is navigating social interactions. So, the conversation must go deeper than that: we need to build up the self-esteem of children brick by brick, teach them to speak up for what they want and to not accept crappy treatment from others and that over time, practicing self-esteem will finally lead to the real-deal.

Let's raise *Confident As Fu*k* kids and get to the heart of bullying: the lack of self-esteem in both the child being bullied and the one doing the bullying. Anyone reading this has lived enough of a life to understand that bullies take advantage of the seemingly "weak." We need to raise warriors who, like Sarah's friend, simply will not tolerate it.

PART

6

IN CONVERSATION
WITH MARK LEARY

"Most of the problems that we face in life — both our personal problems and the problems that plague society — stem from human behavior. Some of our problems arise from our own thoughts, emotions, and actions, and some are due to the behaviors of other people. But in either case, most problems are people problems. Given that's the case, improving the quality of our lives requires a deeper understanding of human behavior, which offers insights into ourselves and others, as well as ideas for ways in which our problems might be solved."

- Mark Leary, Ph.D.

Mark Leary, Ph.D. is a social and personality psychologist who has studied, written about, and taught courses on motivation, emotion, self-awareness, social relationships, and psychological well-being for more than 40 years. Having retired from Duke University in 2019, he continues to work on a variety of projects, many of which focus on writing, speaking, and blogging about human behavior for the general public.

ELLE: People often link confidence and self-esteem together. But there is a distinction you mentioned that you can be confident to execute certain behaviors, but you still might not have high self-esteem. For example, you can be confident to get straight A's in school but then you still don't feel good about yourself. I'd love to hear more about that distinction.

MARK: Confidence, the way I use the term, is related to my estimated likelihood of achieving whatever the goal is, whether it's getting an A in school, making friends, or giving a talk that people will like; it's an estimate of the probability of success. Of course, the higher the estimate of success, the more motivated you'll be to do the behavior and stick with the behavior. All of our behaviors are motivated by the expectancy that we might be able to actually *do* a thing. If you have a low probability of doing it, why bother? Confidence is a sense of efficacy or the ability to accomplish a particular goal. Self-esteem has much more to do with "What do I feel like my value is, particularly in the eyes of the people whose opinions I care about?" Do I believe I have relational or social value to other people, so that when I achieve things or I am a good person, or I'm successful at things, my value to other people increases and I feel good about myself, and that is motivating. but that is separate from whether I think I can get things done. There's a lot of people who are excellent at what they do. They know they're excellent at what they do, but they still don't feel that the people around them sufficiently value them.

ELLE: Well, could that be the case because they are just hanging around with the wrong people?

MARK: There's a lot of different reasons. One is, they could be really successful with things that truly nobody cares about. You could have confidence that you could be the best builder of ships in a bottle. And there are some people who really like that, but most people say, "Well, why are you building ships in a bottle?" And so, it's not really increasing your relational value. It could be that your skills are not appreciated by your particular peer group. And if you were with a different peer group, they would think this was really cool and you would feel accepted and you would feel good about yourself. But in any case, people can do very well and have low self-esteem. You can have some people also who are not particularly successful with things; for example, they are C students or they don't have the best job, but they are surrounded by people who just think they are a great person, and like to spend time with them and want to have relationships with them, and their self-esteem can be very high. Now, there's a correlation between confidence and self-esteem because normally confident people are doing things better, and normally people who do things better are usually more valued by other people. There is a correlation, but there's no necessary connection between a sense of confidence and a sense of self-esteem.

ELLE: Is it always the case that someone has high self-esteem but they may not have confidence? That seems a little bit off, right? I can see where you can be confident but not have self-esteem, but do people who have high self-esteem also have confidence? Even if it's just the confidence in their self-esteem?

MARK: Yes, again there's going to be a correlation. If I feel good about myself, it's probably partly because I am able to do things that people value more successfully. But I do think that if you are adored and everybody just loves having you come to their parties, and they all seek you out, and everybody wants to be your friend, and you're just a nice moral, wonderful friend, you could have exceptionally high self-esteem even though you don't do anything particularly well except be a good friend, and you don't have that much confidence. Maybe you're not doing well in school, and you're not a good public speaker, and you're not making a lot of money, and you don't feel like you can play a good game of golf, you don't have much confidence in things, but if you are surrounded by people who value you, you can feel really good about yourself anyway. Ideally, people's confidence should be calibrated to their actual level of ability. We always say we want people to have confidence, but it doesn't make any sense if they have confidence in something that really they have no likelihood of executing.

ELLE: Yes. Unrealistic confidence. A false or misguided sense of confidence.

MARK: That's right. You are just going to pursue the wrong activities and you're going to experience a life full of disappointment and failure. So you'd like your confidence to be calibrated to the actual probability of success. The problem is that there's no way for any of us to know for sure. What's the probability that if I worked hard enough I could achieve a particular goal? When we have confidence, we're kind of making it up in a way based just on our behavior and our performance and we are listening to what other people are saying about how well we are doing and what our prospects are for success, and we come to this estimate of the probability of doing something successfully, but it's really just a guesstimate. And a lot of times, of course, we underestimate our chances of success, so I may have really low confidence about something, but confident enough to feel that if I stuck with it, I would absolutely achieve it. And there are cases where we have a lot more confidence than we should, and we beat our head against the wall and never get there. The confidence piece, ideally, has to be calibrated, but we often misjudge in one direction or the other. Self-esteem is pretty much based upon our sense of value as a human being, particularly to other people, but we misperceive that too. Sometimes there are plenty of people who everybody likes just fine but they don't feel it themselves. Their self-esteem is low. There are also a lot of people who feel really, really good about themselves—even more than they probably should, as weird as that sounds.

ELLE: I just feel that deep down inside, if a person who lacks integrity in their life, regardless of confidence or projected self-esteem, somewhere inside in their subconscious they are not totally cool with themselves, even if they're portraying it on the outside. Do you know what I mean?

MARK: That very well could be. We never know for sure what people are thinking, and I'm talking here mostly about what people really feel rather than what they show, because sometimes we show more confidence than we have, and it's an important self-presentational thing. You don't want to be going into an athletic contest with your teammates and say, "Man, I think I'm going to really suck today." There are some presentational elements to that. I'm talking mostly here about what people really think about their likelihood of success, and what they really think about their value and their self-esteem. And we are not necessarily good judges. People have to take their confidence and their self-esteem with a grain of salt.

We are all kind of making it up on the basis of the cues and the information that we have about ourselves, which are incomplete, and partial, and biased. And when you really succeed at a something, then you say, "Okay, now I've done it." Now you know that you can do it. But on the road to doing that, confidently working on something you haven't attained yet, and now you're just making a guess, and it's an important guess. You want to be as accurate as you can be, but people have to realize that their confidence is not reality. Your estimate of the probability that if I work real hard, I can become a prize-winning whatever. Now, maybe, maybe not. Try to make the best estimate you can and follow it, but you can't take it your estimate too seriously.

ELLE: Well, and in my opinion you need to build the self-esteem. You can have the confidence first—even if it's a false sense of confidence. For example, I am a writer that has never written a documentary, and someone came to me and said, "I need a writer for this documentary." And I could have said, "Oh no, I have never written a documentary, I don't know how, I am not sure I can do it." Instead I instantly said to myself, "You know what? You are a writer. You'll figure it out. If you are a writer, then you should be able to write anything." I saw it as a challenge, not as something that was not in my repertoire. Confident people often see challenges in a positive light, rather than, "Oh no, what if I fail at this and ruin my reputation?" I never had that moment. But I had the self-esteem and enough confidence to say, "I think I can do it and if I can't, I will gracefully bail out, but

I am going to try it."***** The prospect of a new writing challenge and the project itself outweighed any hesitancy that I had about writing something I have never attempted to write. And in accomplishing that goal, I became even more confident in my creative writing skills. Clearly, you need both, or at the very least you need some modicum of confidence to even develop the self-esteem within whatever it is you're pursuing, if that makes sense.

MARK: Absolutely. It makes sense. And that's a great example, because there's a funny distinction here, between confidence about doing something and confidence in pursuing something. So if I just said, "How confident are you that you could actually write this screenplay?" You might've said, "I don't know, but I am confident that I have the ability to work on this and potentially build the ability and the confidence." There's something different about the confidence "that I can do it right now" versus "I'm confident I can work toward it," and people don't always make that distinction. I think kids in particular, they don't have confidence sometimes unless they can actually do it well now, and often that is not the important thing. The important thing is your projection for the future. Are you confident you can improve on this and potentially do it in the future?

ELLE: Basically, are you confident that you can learn a thing?

. . . .

* **Editor's note:** In fact, this is exactly what I did to land the job of editor for this book! Elle reached out to me one day asking if I knew any good editors for a project she was working on; I've been an editor and in the publishing industry for a decade, but had never edited a book before. I responded, "Well, I've never edited an entire book, but that's just semantics. I'm a good editor and I'd love to help you out!" And just like that, A Confident as F*ck partnership was born.

MARK: Right.

ELLE: We're talking a lot about the world around us and the feedback we get from other people. I'm imagining a scenario though, where there's someone who may only be receiving feedback from strangers or people on social media. Perhaps they don't have a lot of friends, or family or a tribe of people to encourage them, and they are in a profession with minimal praise, but that person still feels good about who they are? Do you really need feedback from close people to have self-esteem? Is that a determining factor?

MARK: I don't know if you would need explicit feedback, but I think you do need to have the sense that you have characteristics that are valued by other people. It's hard for me to imagine somebody having high self-esteem if they don't believe that they have socially valued characteristics. They wouldn't have to be ability characteristics, they could be the characteristics of being a good conversationalist, or a funny person, or cool to hang around with, or having integrity as you mentioned before. It's hard for me to imagine that somebody could have legitimately high self-esteem if they don't think they have any characteristics that are potentially valued by other people.

ELLE: So, ideally you need at least one or two people out there who feel like you are of value.

MARK: And that's sometimes all it takes. You are not trying to please the whole world, you just need to have a support group around you. And if you think about where this whole mechanism came from, through millions years of human evolution, we needed mechanisms to make us behave in ways that gave us a solid position in our little clan, because we were nomadic hunters and gatherers wandering around southern for central Africa for millions of years. You have to do something to be in the good graces of the clan, because if you don't, you don't have people to take care of you. If you break the rules and nobody values you, they may even leave you behind because you are an impediment to the success of the group.

We are designed to try to do things that make us a valuable member, a valuable friend, a valuable team member. And it doesn't take too many people to value us, to give us the social support we need, and the help that we need, and the social connections that we need. And a lot of people in today's society, because they can present themselves to millions of people on the Internet, just keep on seeking more and more and more of that kind of validation. In the old days, there was really only a handful of people whose acceptance and support you cared about.

ELLE: Seeking validation and feedback from strangers on the internet is more vacant and shallow compared to what we are talking about, which is a close member of your family or tribe. I have noticed in my life that confident people—even if they exude it falsely—are trusted. They are dependable. We feel comfortable in their presence because they have a sense of self-assuredness about a thing and about themselves. It is very attractive. Explain the attractiveness of someone with high self-esteem and confidence and why we are drawn to these people.

MARK: I think we're drawn to them because, throughout

most of human history when people were confident, they had some reason to be. I mean, some people are overly confident, but generally speaking. Confidence needs to be calibrated to our abilities, and confident people are confident because they can get things done, whether it's hunting or starting a new business. Confidence is more often than not a reflection of something. It's not a bad idea to hitch your wagon to a star, as the saying goes. You need to make a connection with a confident person. Forming social connections with a confident person is more likely to have a payoff for you because they are going to get more things done, and get more resources. Confidence is often a reflection of actual accomplishment and success and ability, and the more of those people we have around us, the better off we are going to fare. And that's another reason why most of us want to *appear* confident. That's why it's important for us to look confident even when we're not, because we know it's attractive to other people. It shows that we have some kind of resources that other people might find useful and that's going to attract them to us. Again, whether that's social confidence, or it's financial confidence, or just task-based confidence, it indicates that a person has something to offer.

ELLE: Sure. And it seems as though we would say most leaders are confident. For example, when there's a problem with something most people want to throw a confident person at it, because you know they are going to get that shit done on time - they are on it. You don't have to keep asking. They are reliable. People know that about me. For example, if I am not on time for some odd reason, people will immediately get worried because I am always on time. Self-esteem plus confidence; I feel like if you have both, you are more reliable, you are more trustworthy, more able. These are really important factors to have in relationships.

MARK: Absolutely. And people like that have higher self-esteem because it is so socially valued to be trusted, to get things done, to be on time. Other people value that. Self-esteem is just all part sort of a package of having value to other people and providing value to the group.

ELLE: There are so many ways one can work on developing self-esteem, from doing past trauma work, forgiveness, even surrounding yourself with new people. There are a ton of life-hacks as to how someone could go forward in developing self-esteem and inner confidence.

MARK: People who chronically have low self-esteem, who don't feel as good about themselves as they should, differ in a number of ways from each other. I think the antidote for low self-esteem depends on what the problem is to begin with.

We sometimes lump all low self-esteem people in the same bucket, and then we come up with an intervention to try to help them. And I think we need to do a better job of identifying the source of their low self-esteem. And I haven't thought about this before, but this would apply to confidence as well. If I lacked confidence, it matters whether I really don't have the skills and I lack confidence. That's much different than having the skills, but not being able to see them.

ELLE: Not too long ago I overheard a very smart person with a PhD. say to someone else, "The thing is, I really know my stuff, I'm just not confident." It's interesting because the statement of "I really know my stuff" is a very confident statement, yet they struggle with being confident in putting themselves out there.

MARK: That's an interesting case; it's not lack of confidence in their ability but in their presentation of the knowledge or their marketing of it to other peopleHow many times have we said to someone, "You are so great, you are so smart, I don't understand why you don't see this?" Words don't budge the needle for some people struggling with self-confidence.

Particularly if you have had an entire childhood and adolescence of negative, abusive, unaccepting parents and peer groups. So now you're 30 years old and your self-esteem is not going to budge easily. There was an interesting study done of social anxiety a number of years ago where they had these highly-socially anxious male college students who were afraid to talk to women. They probably all had low self-esteem. I mean, because that correlates highly with being very shy.

They did a study where what they told the participants to simply have conversations with six other participants over the next hour for five or 10 minutes each. But these women that he would talk to were actually research accomplices, and they were trained to be really positive and affirming; not over the top, but acting like they were interested in what the guy was saying and doing. And this one hour of experiences talking to six different women, all of whom seemed to enjoy talking to him, caused not only at the moment his self-esteem to go up, but these men became less socially anxious even three months later.

ELLE: That's really interesting. In this book, I talk about someone who went from ground zero with extreme debilitating shyness to the point where in their mid-30s, they hired a social coach who would take them out to a mall or crowded public place and help them study people a little bit before making a plan to walk up and talk to the cashier at the record store or just have conversations with shoppers and strangers etc. And once you have practiced it and realized, "Okay, that wasn't so bad. No one hit me. No one punched me in the face. No one told me to fuck off," it sparks a little bit more confidence and can feed itself as you continue to put yourself out there. And the person is getting used to the fact that they didn't get rejected.

MARK: And most people are generally nice. There are a few places in the country this wouldn't be true, but most of the time people are generally at least pleasant.

ELLE: What are some other things that you found interesting along your studies and writing with regards to self-esteem and self-love?

MARK: Yes, absolutely. We have been talking about self-confidence, and the probability of being successful. Self-esteem is, how good do I feel about myself based on how much value I think I have. The other thing I studied is self-compassion, which is something altogether different. Traditionally, we lumped a whole lot of things into the label of self-esteem, which included when people sort of acted like it was self-love. But it's pretty clear now that that's not a good way to think about what self-esteem is. Self-compassion is how kindly and nicely do you treat yourself no matter what. This isn't how much you like yourself, it is not the probability of whether you are going to do well. Self-compassion is, do you treat yourself as nicely when things go wrong as you would treat your best friend when they have things go wrong.

Self-compassion is to take your shortcomings in stride. Everybody has shortcomings. Everybody fails. You don't like them, you're not saying, "Well, it's perfectly okay that I failed the class." But you just don't catastrophize and internalize those shortcomings or mistakes. And this is somewhat independent of self-esteem and self-confidence.

Do I treat myself as nicely as I treat my loved ones? This is something a little more like self-love but sometimes self-love can be described as just love yourself because you are a human being. And yeah, we all should love and accept ourselves, but this is something a little bit more actionable. What am I feeling? How am I treating myself?

ELLE: Self-compassion sounds better anyway, more clear and encompassing. And it doesn't have the sort of the new age, hippie-dippie feel to it that can turn people off. And we all go through that. Even the most confident people among us with high self-esteem have moments of, "Who the hell do I think I am with this thing I'm doing?" Or sometimes I have put my foot in my mouth and I think "Well, that was regrettable but it's just a blip and you can't win them all." Those experiences are also great platforms for growth and learning.

MARK: Exactly. The lesson is: people who have the lowest self-esteem probably discriminate least well about whether or not they ought to take something to heart. For example, my parents often gave me this line: "Don't care what other people think. Just march to your own drummer and don't care what other people think at all." As a social psychologist, I think that is just terrible advice. We wouldn't want to live in a world where nobody cared about what anybody else thought about them. It would be terrible. What I try to teach my kids, and I don't know if I'm successful, is to discriminate. When you get negative feedback from other people or other people don't seem to like you, try to figure out if it matters. Most of the time, it really doesn't matter what this person thinks. We have an automatic reaction to negative feedback. And I make an evolutionary argument here. In that little group of 30 to 50 people back in nomadic times, everybody's opinions of you mattered. Everybody in your clan - their opinion of you mattered. The problem is we don't have just 30 people anymore. We have the whole world wide web.

ELLE: Another good one: a peripheral family member had written my brother and I the same horrible, mean-spirited letter on Facebook. My brother called and warned me, saying, "Hey, so-and-so sent us a horrible letter on Facebook. It is so bad, don't even read it." And I said, "Thank you so much for telling me. Don't tell me one more thing or hint at anything about that letter; I am going to delete it and I do not want that negative energy." I went onto Facebook and even covered my eyes a bit for fear that I might see even the first line of the letter...and I deleted it. I have told a bunch of people that story and not one person told me they would have been able to control not reading it. That is sad to me. They could control it. They could delete or just press block in these types of situations but they don't.

MARK: I think that's magnificent and such a message for your book, to be able to do that. Part of the attraction in reading that stuff for a lot of people is "I need to know the full details of what people are saying about me and how much they dislike me." And I understand that to some degree, but a lot of times you really don't need to know. I think that was brilliant reaction and I admire that.

ELLE: I had the benefit of being warned, of course, by someone else who had already read it. Whereas I might have been sucked right into that trap. But luckily my brother saved one other person, me, from feeling the way he felt after he read that letter.

MARK: I think a lot of people don't not even consider the price they are paying to receive that type of constant, unwarranted feedback. There is something to be said there, and it is critically important to have it articulated.

Our lives are filled with many challenges. All of us struggle with personal problems such as stress, anxiety, depression, self-doubt, addiction, and worries about our health, finances, and future. Our relationships with our partners, children, and other family members are often riddled with conflict, and our relationships with our friends, neighbors, bosses, and co-workers are challenging as well. Society heaps on additional concerns in the form of crime, violence, economic problems, prejudice, political discord, terrorism, and environmental issues.

All of these problems are complex, and their solutions elusive. Yet they share a common link. For the most part, they are all caused by human beings. Most of the problems that we face — within ourselves, in our relationships with other people, and in society — are caused by people. Granted, a few problems don't require human collusion (tornadoes and earthquakes come to mind), but most do. Human behavior is by far the single largest cause of the difficulties that each of us experience in life. Most problems are people problems, and the people who cause our problems are quite often us.

- **Mark Leary Ph.D. from** *Psychology Today*

PART 7

CONFIDENT AS FU*K CONCLUSIONS

In order to be *Confident As Fu*k*, you must:

* Deal with lingering shame
* Tackle unhealthy addictions
* Get physically and mentally healthy
* Get rid of or minimize contact with toxic, negative downers
* Make friends with confident people with high self-esteem
* Learn to be vulnerable
* Stop people-pleasing
* Be authentic with your words and actions
* Be consistently gratefulWish others well
* Encourage and help others to succeed
* Be happy for the success of others
* Be inspired by the success of others
* Stop being a victim
* Get a life coach or therapist—or both!
* Take risks and leaps of faith
* Overcome shyness
* Learn about the power of your subconscious mindStop rescuing people
* Help the worthy, not the needy
* Stop having NONversations

* Choose your battles wisely

* Stop being a downer, with words and thoughts

* Learn to interpret and translate your emotional indicators

* Call people on their shit—and call yourself on your own shit

* Receive and give constructive criticism

* Speak up in all areas of your life

As you move forward on your journey to becoming *Confident As Fu*k*, ask yourself these questions:

* What negative patterns, situations, or people keep appearing in my life that I do not like and wish were different?

* Is there something about my mother/father/caretaker's parenting that I disapprove of in hindsight? What are they, and are these disappointments correlated to or mirroring any areas of my life that create discord and unhappiness within me now?

* What has been disappointing about the romantic relationships that I have had? Do I see any of these undesirable dating characteristics in my upbringing, past, or childhood?

* Is there anything I wish I could change about my employment experiences?

* What negative stories or labels were declared about me by my parents, family, teachers, and friends? Did I adopt any of their labels and stories? If so, how has one of those stories or labels kept me from self-esteem and success? Are any of these stories and labels true? Do I really believe these things about myself?

* Is the story I am about to tell worthwhile and helpful, or am I just adding negativity into the world?

* What kind of reaction do I think I will get if I share my excitement with this person? Do I really need this person to be supportive of me, or can I just keep this to myself or share it with someone else who is really on my team? Why am I feeling the need to be correct in this moment? Can I unpack why that is so important to me?

* How am I feeling after this phone call, dinner, hang-out, trip? If I am not feeling good, why not? What transpired during this interaction that put me off kilter?

* Am I really going to let the past shape my future or am I gonna get off this motherfucking train to hell right now?

Becoming *Confident As Fu*k* is an all-encompassing enterprise in embodying high self-esteem and self-confidence. It begins with your thoughts about yourself and the actions you take. You might need assistance in navigating shyness and low self-esteem, or help in learning and practicing vulnerability and receiving, but it is attainable for all of us. While being *Confident As Fu*k* is also about reaching the point where *other people's opinions of you are none of your business*, let's be reasonable: we all live in a world where other people's opinions have value. No one is going to hire you if you have a reputation as an unreliable employee or if you are bad at a service you are providing (I am certainly not going to return to an inept massage therapist for another massage). If you keep running into the same problems and criticisms from others, then yes, you have some self-examination to do in order to prevent that from happening again. Being *Confident as Fu*k* is not about completely ignoring on *every level* what people think of you. Instead it's about not letting downers affect your self-esteem when it comes from a place of nonconstructive, unsupportive criticism.

We are all great at some things and not so great at others. We are all striving to be happy in all areas of our lives: health, abundance, love, and career. We all want improvement and our work is never finished.

For those of you who already feel *Confident As Fu*k,* I urge you to check some classic alpha pitfalls in the name of refining and evolving your already high levels of self-esteem. *Confident As Fu*k* people are leaders, and we must continue to cheerlead and encourage others to reach their own heights of greatness, while remembering to extract lessons from them as well. There are always great rewards in paying it forward.

Being *Confident As Fu*k* is not about walking around telling everyone you are confident as fuck. I am not advocating a showy display or announcement to the world. This is about moving through your life feeling happy and proud of yourself and who you are in this world, and who you are still becoming. When you are truly *Confident As Fu*k* it emanates from you naturally, because it is *who you are.*

I wish for all of you a *Confident As Fu*k* life.

ABOUT THE AUTHOR

ELLE RUSS is the author of *Confident As Fu*k* and best-selling thyroid book *The Paleo Thyroid Solution*. She is a leading voice in the Paleo, Primal, and Ancestral Health Movements. Elle began her writing career in sketch comedy, and is an alumna of the world-famous comedy theater, *The Second City – Chicago*, and a main company alumna of the renowned *Acme Comedy Theater* in Hollywood. Elle wrote and performed in more than 100 live sketch comedy and improv shows. Her writing resumé includes books, articles, and TV/film scripts including the award-winning documentary *Headhunt Revisited*. Elle is also the host of the popular *Primal Blueprint Podcast*, a top-ranked show created by New York Times Bestselling author Mark Sisson. Elle lives and plays in Southern California.

THE PALEO THYROID SOLUTION

By Elle Russ

The Paleo Thyroid Solution dispels outdated, conventional thyroid wisdom still practiced by uninformed doctors and provides the in-depth guidance necessary to solve hypothyroidism, achieve vibrant health, and optimize thyroid fat-burning hormone metabolism. Over 200 million people worldwide and 20+ million Americans have some form of thyroid disease, but 60% are undiagnosed and unaware of their condition.

Available world-wide here:
Primal Blueprint (publisher)
Kobo
Amazon.com

ISBN 978-1-9395-6324-8
$21.95 USD
Published Sept. 8, 2016
6 × 9 Inches · 300 Pages
Paperback, Ebook